TOTALLY SCALLOPS

Not just another cookbook

Judy Eberspaecher

Introduction by Alex Eberspaecher

Kimagic Publishing

Library and Archives Canada Cataloguing in Publication

Eberspaecher, Judy, 1943-
    Totally scallops : not just another cookbook / Judy Eberspaecher.

Includes index.
ISBN 978-0-9783549-9-2

    1. Cookery (Scallops). I. Title.

TX753.E23 2009   641.6'94   C2009-905985-1

Production Credits
Cover and interior design: Igor Kravtchenko, KiMagic
Front cover photo: Igor Kravtchenko
Back cover photo: Alex Eberspaecher
Author photo: Gary Crallé
Interior photography: Judy Eberspaecher, except as noted

First Published by KiMAGIC 2009
Printed in China

I dedicate this book to Alex, who supported me throughout this whole process with his advice, his love and many glasses of wine.

In memory of Gerry Rice.

Geography of Recipes

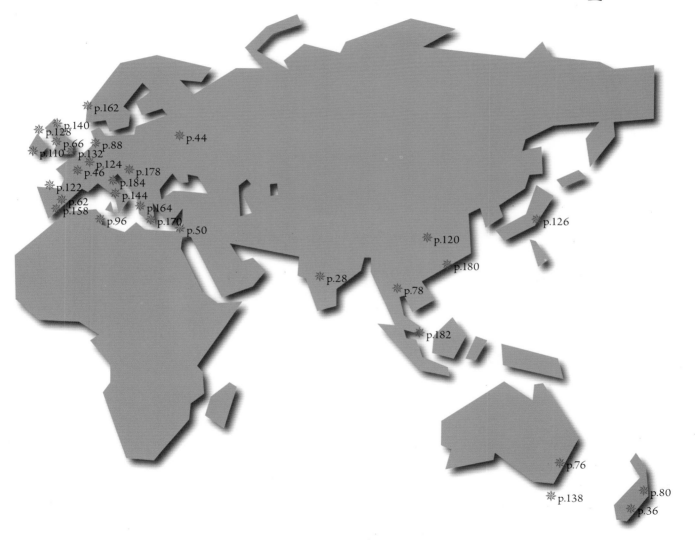

Table of Contents

Scallop Draggers in Digby Harbour

Acknowledgements

The dream of writing this book began in the mid 80's when my late friend, Gerry Rice, made many trips from Digby, Nova Scotia to Oakville, Ontario with a hundred pounds of frozen scallops for my friends and me to enjoy. I collected their favorite recipes and vowed that one day I would write a scallop cookbook. After seeing those bits of paper in my cupboard for over 20 years I was on the verge of throwing them out when I told my husband Alex what my intentions had been. From that point onward, he would not let the idea die. He found a publisher and has encouraged me in every adventure this project has taken me, as have my sons, Stefan and Andrew. Needless to say, without Alex, there would not have been a book.

Scallops had been a regular item on my parents' menu when I was growing up so I took them for granted, coming from 'scallop territory' in Nova Scotia. Naturally a scallop cookbook is a collection of recipes; I soon found out that many people knew very little about these creatures so the dream of a cookbook turned into a scallop nightmare! The more I researched, the more there was to learn and verify so, when I was offered the chance to spend a few days on the Royal Fundy on the Bay of Fundy, courtesy of the Bedford Institute of Oceanography and O'Neil Fishery Ltd., Digby, I jumped at the chance. This was an adventure of a lifetime and I hope the research scientists and the crew were not sorry they took me aboard.

To Mark Lundy, Senior Research Technician, I want to say thanks for answering all of my questions, some more bluntly than I expected ("What are those round red creatures called?") and for editing my information. To Amy Glass, thanks for letting me share the Doghouse and late night stories while anchored at 45° 09' 337"N and 65° 38' 836" W. Thanks to Donnie Ross who explained endlessly the technology of running the boat and impressed me so much, that was, until he left me in the wheelhouse and went below with the boat steaming full ahead! Thanks to Joey Specht who allowed me to take over his galley and cook for everyone. What nerve, I cooked fish for fishermen! Thanks to Kevin O'Connell who took the chance and let me run the gear and was not upset with the mess I made, even when he had to climb the boom to grab that hook I let go! These people are among the kindest and most patient I have ever met. After trying to do this work, I have a new respect for fishermen and people who travel the seas. This was truly one of the high points of my life when it comes to adventure, even with all the bruises from being bashed against the equipment!

I could not have written a book about scallops throughout the five continents without the helpful and generous chefs who prepared wonderful dishes, fed me in their kitchens and gave me their treasured recipes: Chef Lee Miller from Penguin Isle Restaurant in Nags Head, North Carolina; Chef Claude AuCoin from Digby Pines, Nova Scotia; Pia Carroll and Sinclair Philip from Sooke Harbour House, Vancouver Island; Michael Blackie from Brookstreet Hotel, Ottawa; Robert Clark, C Restaurant, Vancouver; Patrick McMurray, Robert Pendergast and Sean Berabioff of Starfish Restaurant in Toronto; Executive Chef Theo Randall, The InterContinental, London, UK; Chef Greg Hopkins, Croc's 19th Street Bistro, Virginia Beach, Virginia; Pamela Barefoot, Malfa, Virginia: my son Stefan and "Nana" Schofield from Tasmania; Jacques Marie, Toronto; Dr. Michael Lim, Singapore; Marimar Torres, Marimar Estate Vineyards & Winery, California; and Yannick Ouellet, Gaspé Bay (Gaspésie). I cannot forget my friends from more than twenty years ago who willingly shared their favorite recipes with me and sparked the idea for the book in the beginning.

Among the others who helped make this venture possible and enjoyable are Sandra Phinney, Yarmouth, Nova Scotia; Randy Brooks and Kristen Pickett, Nova Scotia Tourism; Melvin Thomas, Thistle Down Country Inn, Digby; Brian Hartz, Bakers Journal, Ontario; Gary Crallé, Georgetown, Ontario; Lexa Betson, Vancouver; Aaron Tuell, Outer Banks Visitors Bureau, Manteo and Karen Warlitner, Nags Head, North Carolina; Craig Fancy, Fancy's Jewellers, Nova Scotia; Tamara Vasquez and Diego Errazuriz, Santa Alicia Winery, Chile; Lorraine King and Colin Evans, Swansea, Wales; Laura Casado and Eva Bertran, Sonoma, California; Laura Wood Haber, Virginia Beach; Rob Saunders, Island Scallops Ltd., British Columbia; Ghislain Boudreau, Iles de la Madeleine, Quebec and Maria Wrazen, London, England. Thanks to my sons: Andrew for sharing his expertise and giving me technical assistance, and Stefan for reading the manuscript and offering constructive criticism. I am indebted to my brother, Eric Hiltz, and my friend, Nancy Smith, for combing through the text and pinpointing those small but important changes. Special thanks must go to Igor, my publisher who spent many 'hours of darkness' designing and producing something that we both like.

The most fun in writing a book that contains recipes is enjoying the prepared dishes. I have to say thanks to my testers: Eric and Shirley Hiltz; Jocelyn and Peter Okens; Jim and Veronica Bradt; The Kravtchenko Family; Laurie Gluck; Peter and Lauryn McLelland; Glen and Tineke Ruppel; Shirley and Raymond Kennedy; The Tomlin Family and my number one tester and taster, my husband and best friend, Alex, who enjoyed scallops whether he wanted to or not!

Mark Lundy, Biologist with Fisheries and Oceans, Canada.

Cultivated scallops are suspended on lines hung from these platforms in Spain. Photo by: Lawrence Barton

Introduction

Legend has it that the goddess Aphrodite arrived on earth on the shell of a scallop. The exact time is somewhat shrouded in the uncertainties of ancient history, but modern scholars believe that it was during the 12th or 13th century BC, about the time of the Trojan War. I'm not sure if it is because of my modesty, or political correctness that I don't wish to elaborate much further on the details of the voluptuous and scantily-clad goddess. I will only suggest that much later on we dedicated the word *aphrodisiac* in her honour. In any case, it is the scallop we are fascinated with, not the lady.

Scallops, or at least a part of scallops, have remained with us throughout the ages and through many different cultures. They have become a welcomed and healthy food on our table, not forgetting that it also puts food on the table of the thousands of fishermen worldwide who often chance the most inhospitable conditions on the seas during their quest of the little critters. Scallops are found naturally in almost all the world's oceans and in those waters that are not suitable, man is trying his best to establish scallop farms, often with varying degrees of success. Some Asian countries have a thriving farming industry and although in taste they cannot compete with wild scallops, there are exceptions. In order to preserve the plentiful and healthy wild stocks, farming has been quite successful and even the best of palates would have great difficulties distinguishing between the farmed variety from those found in the wild.

In Canada scallops occur naturally in the east and the west with the largest fishery in the North Atlan-

tic off Nova Scotia. In the USA we find them along the north-eastern states to North Carolina as well as Alaska. Norway plays an important role in supplying the European markets as do the British Isles. France, Britain and Spain too have wild stocks, although the latter two are turning more to farming. China and Japan, Iceland, Australia, Scotland, Chile, Peru, Argentina and New Zealand are all important players while Asia, Chile and Spain are in the forefront of the scallop culturing industry.

Generally, the best sites for scallop cultivation are those where there are good currents and temperatures are between 10ºC (50ºF) and 17ºC (63ºF) for the maximum length of time. Summer temperatures above 20ºC (68ºF) and winter temperatures below 4ºC (40ºF) can be stressful to scallops.

Curiously enough, within the Mediterranean Region where it all began, and the Romans followed the Greeks in discovering this bivalve, they are still found in the Mediterranean Sea but there is no longer a viable commercial harvest. Nor can we find a workable yield of scallops in the warm waters of the Caribbean although a small species of wild scallop still can be found. Although scallops are not harvested commercially in the Caribbean, they are popular with tourists and most restaurants include them on their menu.

There are about 350 identifiable species of scallops worldwide yet no more than a handful are commercially harvested. Some species are too tiny to bother with; others are not very palatable or are too tough to eat while still others are harvested only for their beautiful shells. Of the 350 species known, many are edible and none is believed to be poisonous although from time to time caution is in order as scallops can become inedible and unsafe as a result of foraging on pollutants, both natural, but more recently, by pollutants that are manmade.

The most prevalent species used commercially are the Bay Scallops, the sweetest and the smallest, followed by the Sea Scallops which are the largest. In Europe the Coquille Saint-Jacques Scallop, not to be confused with the popular entrée of Coquille Saint-Jacques, and the Iceland Scallop are most common. Scallops are molluscs that live in a beautiful, well… scallop-shaped shell. Unlike mussels, clams and oysters, they are not confined to the bottom but free-living and can move about in a graceful manner when disturbed or threatened. Generally, the edible part of the scallop is not the whole mollusc itself, but rather the adductor muscle, that tender and fat-free muscle that opens and closes the shell, thus forcing water from the shell and propelling the scallop through the ocean. The reproductive part, known commonly as coral, although savoured in Europe, South America and New Zealand, is not generally offered in North America.

The harvesting of wild and free-living scallops has become a profitable fishery although there are several indications that a few stocks are declining, prompting concerted efforts to protect them. Except for the Calico Scallop in the Atlantic, as a whole, the diverse North American populations are stable and if conservation measures are adhered to, there is no reason to believe that it will not remain so for the foreseeable future. Traditionally the bulk of the scallops are taken during regulated seasons by commercial fishing boats by dragging just above the sea bottom. The scallop is immediately shucked or opened up, the adductor muscle is removed quickly and the shell along with the rest of the mollusc is returned to the sea. The edible part, what we now know as the scallop, is either frozen immediately or put on ice until the scallop dragger, as the ship is called, returns to port.

An alternative method of harvesting scallops, where divers handpick the critters off the seabed, undoubtedly is the same method used two thousand years ago by the Romans. Diver-caught scallops, also referred to as day-boat scallops, are collected by hand, with minimal effects on the surrounding marine environment. The term "day-boat" indicates that the boats carrying the divers return to shore to offload at the end of each day, rather than spending days at sea. Scallops on boats that stay at sea for many days are often treated with preservatives to keep them from spoiling until they are delivered to shore. These preservatives are not necessary on day boats. In shallow waters, they can be gathered while snorkelling or by merely bending and picking them up. The tiny Nantucket Bay Scallops are so prized that residents of Nantucket, Massachusetts, on the east coast of United States, have their own season to gather them for themselves before they can be harvested commercially.

A third method, the culturing of scallops in farms that are established in or near the ocean, predominantly in Asia, Chile and Spain, is gaining in popularity and many of the scallops consumed in the United States, come from these farms. There are several methods in use. More often than not, the juvenile scallops are raised in hatcheries and then suspended on long lines using fine netting. The contraption is then moved out to the open sea to grow into a harvestable size in about 18 months. Giving credit to mankind's ingenuity, a number of other methods are also experimented with. One technique involves drilling holes in the shell and hanging the scallop from it and another one uses waterproof adhesives. Whatever method of raising scallops in a controlled environment is used, it is less controversial than raising salmon in pens, as the scallop feeds itself with the natural food sources from the sea.

If pearls are a girl's best friend, eat more scallops. These pearls might be smaller than those found by the divers in giant oysters in the depths of the Indian Ocean or the South China Sea, but they are nevertheless still an object of beauty. Found occasionally in just about any type of shellfish, both in fresh and saltwater, our scallops are no exception. There is probably no commercial harvest of scallop pearls anywhere because of their rarity, but those that are found frequently, and yes even in North America, are sold by the crew of the fishing trawlers to local jewellery shops for processing into objects of beauty and rarity.

If pearls are a metaphor for beauty and the succulent white meat of the scallop's muscle is one of the most delicious and healthy foods discovered by mankind, just think what a glass or two of Champagne would do. For that you must go to a separate section in the book. Back in the days of the Goddess Aphrodite, Champagne wasn't even invented yet but then again, a few scallops and a few strings of pearls were probably enough.

Alex Eberspaecher

Your Personal Notes

Wine with Scallops

Wine With Scallops

Advice from Alex Eberspaecher
wine writer, judge, educator and taster but above all, a lover of food and wine

It would be false to proclaim that we have found the perfect wine to go with scallops. The very same would be true of course with all foods. Beef, for instance is a rather simple and bland tasting dish until we add spices or sauces. It is the seasoning that permits us to find a well-matched wine. The same is true for scallops, in fact for all seafood. Much has been written about the myth of matching seafood with white wine only, while others are advocating that red wine with fish is just fine. Of course it is. Our rules are simple and although they may be going against established conventions, they work.

Never use a wine for cooking or as a companion with your food that you would not drink on its own.

This first rule, especially when wine is also used in the preparation of the recipe, is perhaps the most important one. After all wine enhances food and you would only ruin the food if you use an inferior wine.

Drink any wine you like; any colour, any country and any grape will do as long as you enjoy it.

The second rule is still simpler. If you wish to become an expert in matching food with wine, or the other way around, there is a simple test. Take a bite of your food and then take a sip of wine. If you can taste the wine **and** food in your mouth, you have created the perfect match. If on

the other hand you can taste only the wine or only the food, one is overpowering the other. The wine should not overpower your scallops nor should the scallops overpower the wine.

Rules about wines are not etched in stone. As each recipe will taste different because of the herbs, spices and sauces we use to prepare the scallops, matching each dish with the perfect wine would fill a book by itself. However, to make it as easy as possible, we will share some of our wines we have enjoyed, perhaps at times more than we should have, during the preparation of the dishes featured in this book.

If there is one wine that will go with every scallop dish, it would be a ***sparkling wine***. Champagne, as the wine is called if it comes from the Champagne Region of France, but also all the other sparklers such as Sekt from Germany, Cava from Spain and Prosecco from Italy, are incredibly well-suited to accompany any food. Nothing will prepare your palate better for your food than a glass of cold sparkling wine: before as an aperitif, during the meal with your scallops and afterwards with some dessert and good friends. With the exception of the Italian Spumante, which can be rather sweet, don't worry about the sweetness of your bubbly, in fact a slight sweetness will often make your wine and your meal more pleasurable.

The same holds true for white wine. Perhaps a good ***Riesling*** with its fine and delicate acidity is your best bet. Again, dry is often preferred but we have found that many of the scallop dishes are enhanced with a wine that has a slight sweetness. It is with this purpose that we mention Riesling, **the king of white wines**. There can be little dispute that the Riesling is the very best of the great white wines when used in cooking and as a companion with most foods. No other variety has so many different levels to choose from, from

the sweetest to the driest. This wine has a very delicate, yet still pronounced acidity that goes so well with most foods and especially scallops.

Perhaps you prefer a **Sauvignon Blanc**. With its freshness and herbaceous tastes, this wine goes well with most seafoods and especially shellfish. Always dry in taste, a Sauvignon Blanc comes in many styles. From the very mute one that is almost undistinguishable from other varieties, Sauvignon Blancs will lead us through a medley of tastes ending up with the typical and powerful aromas of gooseberries, fresh-cut grass and other herbs which we find in the wines from New Zealand. Our own choice consisted of wines that fell somewhere in between the extremes.

Another good wine to try with scallops would be a **Muscadet** from the Loire Region of France. This wine has no relationship to the Moscato grape which is usually very fruity and often used to make sweet wines. Unfortunately a good Muscadet is rather difficult to find except in France, but if you do, you will have a winning match. With its light and tangy aroma, decent acidity and tastes that may be slightly salty, it is a perfect match for most seafood dishes.

As a distant next recommendation we suggest **Chardonnay**. Realizing that Chardonnay is still a popular white wine, we also know that its popularity is on the decline. Perhaps we even differ here with your local sommelier, but in our experience a Chardonnay is seldom a great food wine. Of course, rules are meant to be broken and there are some good Chardonnays so we recommend that you pick one that is

fresh and, most importantly, **uno-aked**. We found that the vanilla and tannins found in oaky wines do not go great with scallops.

There are many other white wines that go very well with scallops, especially **Pinot Grigio** and **Pinot Blanc,** but we must not forget the **Gewürztraminer** with its delicious spiciness and the **Muscat Ottonel** which are perfect for any scallop dishes prepared on the grill, especially if there is some smokiness in the taste. One final white wine that will go rather well with scallops and one that is very reasonably priced is the **Vinho Verde** from Portugal. Young, fresh and served well-chilled, a Vinho Verde is low in alcohol and quite refreshing during the hotter summer months.

Almost all **Rosé** wines would go well with scallops as long as they are reasonably dry in taste. One exception would be the blush Zinfandels from California. We found them best to be enjoyed on their own and not with seafood.

Red wines are more difficult to match with scallop dishes. Our recommendation here is that you stay with the lighter ones and leave the complex and heavy reds for later. A nice fruity **Beaujolais** or a **Northern Italian Valpolicella or Bardolino** would do well as they have good acidity as would most **Pinot Noirs** except of course the high priced ones from the Burgundy. Leave them for after you eat when you celebrate your successful meal.

With that, you have carte blanche to drink whatever you like because *the best wine is still the wine you like best.*

Your Personal Notes

Appetizers

Raw Sea Scallops on the Half Shell, Starfish Restaurant, Toronto, Canada

Avocado and Scallop Ceviche (Mexico)

Ingredients

¾ **pound (375 g) raw scallops finely chopped**
½ **cup (125 g) fresh lime juice**
3 tbsp. peanut oil or vegetable oil
24 red peppercorns, crushed
1 large ripe avocado, peeled
2 tbsp. fresh chives, chopped
40 small white mushrooms
¼ **cup (75 ml) vegetable oil**
2 tbsp. fresh lemon juice
1 medium garlic clove, peeled and crushed
salt and pepper to taste

Method

Combine the lime juice, oil, peppercorns, salt and pepper together in a bowl. Stir in the scallops, cover and refrigerate for at least 4 hours while they marinate. They should become opaque in this time. Mash the avocado until almost smooth, then add it along with the chives or scallions to the marinating scallops (do not drain them) and mix well. Set aside for at least ½ hour, refrigerated. About half an hour before serving the scallops, remove the stems from the mushrooms and wipe them to remove any dirt. Combine the vegetable oil, lemon juice, garlic, salt and pepper in a small bowl, and brush the insides of the mushrooms liberally with the mixture. Just before serving, drain the caps and fill with the scallop mixture. Garnish scallop ceviche with additional chives, if desired.
Makes 8 servings.

Store your seafood in the refrigerator if you intend to use it within two days after purchase. In case you will not use your seafood within two days after purchase, wrap it in moisture-proof paper or plastic wrap, placed in a heavy plastic bag, or stored in an air-tight, rigid container, and store it in the freezer. Keep the temperature of the refrigerator between 34° and 40°F (2° and 4°C) and your freezer at 0° to -20°F (-17° to -28°C).

ElDorado Seaside Suites in Mexico and many other resorts serve scallops to their wedding parties.

Barbecued Sea Scallops Wrapped in Prosciutto

Ingredients

2 pounds (1 kg) shelled, large sea scallops
½ pound prosciutto, thinly sliced
½ cup butter, melted
skewers or toothpicks, soaked in water

Method

Preheat grill for medium-high heat. Wrap each scallop with a thin slice of prosciutto, thread on to skewers or secure with a toothpick. Lightly oil grill grate. Arrange scallops on the grill, and baste with butter. Cook for 5 minutes, turn, and baste with butter. Cook for another 8 minutes, or until opaque.
Makes 8 – 12 servings.

Scallops, along with various other foods have been held in the highest regards as aphrodisiacs historically. It is easy to see the sexual attraction of scallops. Their flesh is far milder than many of the ocean's creatures. Their texture is soft - voluptuous on the tongue. Their shells make beautiful serving vessels, and, when served at their freshest, scallops offer a flavour that is the essence of the briny sea.

Appetizers

Barbecued Sea Scallops Wrapped in Prosciutto

Tandoori Scallops (India)

Ingredients

¾ cup (200 ml) plain low-fat yogurt
3 tbsp. lime juice, or lemon juice
1 clove garlic, minced
1 tsp. salt
1/2 tsp. ground ginger
1/4 tsp. ground cumin
1/4 tsp. turmeric
1/4 tsp. curry powder
1 pound (500 g) large sea scallops, fresh or thawed
1 tsp. vegetable oil paprika, to taste

Method

In a non-metallic bowl, combine all ingredients except oil and paprika. Mix well to coat scallops evenly. Cover and refrigerate at least 2 hours, turning scallops occasionally. Preheat broiler or start barbecue. Thread scallops on skewers and brush lightly with oil. Sprinkle with paprika. Broil or barbecue about 4 inches (10cm) from heat source about 8 to 10 minutes, turning frequently.
Makes 4 servings.

What is a Scallop?

The textbook definition says that a scallop is a member of the shellfish family known as bivalves, named for its two valves, or shells. Its upper valve is a mottled colour, occasionally bright yellow, orange or purple, and its lower valve is almost white. The colour, size and shape varies with the species of scallop.

Tandori Scallops on a bed of Rice

Octopus Bacon-Wrapped Scallops (British Columbia)

Robert Clark, C Restaurant, Vancouver

Ingredients

6 large scallops (diver scallops or responsibly farmed)
6 slices octopus bacon* 6 inches (15 cm) long
6 slices foie gras, 1.5 ounces (45 g) each

French Toast:
¼ cup ground hazelnuts
1 tbsp. sugar
1 tbsp. butter
1 egg white
2 tbsp. hazelnut oil
2 whole eggs, beaten
12 slices brioche

Sauce:
1 tbsp. butter
4 whole shallots, thinly sliced
3 small Oregon truffles, thinly sliced
3 tbsp. cognac
3 tbsp. port
1 cup (250 ml) good veal jus
12 cloves garlic confit, cooked in olive oil

Method

Wrap the scallops with the octopus bacon (see attached recipe) or prosciutto, holding it in place with tooth picks or bamboo skewer. Grill or pan sear the scallops to medium rare.

In a food processor, puree the nuts, sugar, and butter. Add the egg white, mix until smooth. Cut the brioche slices into the size and shape you like and make little sandwiches with the nut mixture as the filling. Dip in the beaten eggs and cook as you normally would for French toast.
Sweat the shallots and truffles in the butter for 2 minutes. Add the cognac and port, reduce down until almost dry. Add the veal jus and cooked garlic cloves and bring to a boil. Keep warm.
Season the foie gras and quickly sear on both sides, remove from the pan, but reserve the fat. Wisk the rendered foie fat into the sauce and serve.
Makes 2 – 3 servings.

*This signature dish of Robert Clark of C Restaurant in Vancouver is typically done with Octopus bacon. For the at-home chef who may not have access to Octopus bacon, prosciutto may be used. For the recipes for C's Octopus Bacon, the Veal Jus and Garlic Confit, see the Sauces, Condiments and Extras Section.
*For a quick substitute to brown veal jus, use a good-quality canned sauce or packaged dry brown sauce. If desired, flavour with a small amount of Madeira and red wine.

Chef Robert Clark, C Restaurant, Vancouver, Canada. As part of C's "100 Mile Menu" Qualicum Bay Scallops from Island Scallops are always on the menu.
Photo by Hammit Attie Photography

Empress Hotel in Victoria, British Columbia's capital city

Coconut Scallops (Caribbean)

Ingredients

1 cup (200 g) sweetened flaked coconut
1 cup (250 ml) boiling-hot water
¼ tsp. cayenne
½ tsp. salt
10 medium sea scallops
½ cup (125 ml) all-purpose flour
1 large egg
½ cup (125 ml) vegetable oil
salt and pepper to taste
lime wedges

Method

Preheat oven to 350°F (180°C.) In a small bowl stir together coconut and water. Drain coconut in a sieve and pat dry. On a baking sheet spread coconut in one layer and bake in middle of oven until pale golden, about 10 minutes. In a bowl stir together coconut, cayenne, and salt. Remove tough muscle from side of each scallop if necessary. Pat scallops dry and season with salt and pepper. In two separate shallow bowls have flour and lightly beaten egg ready. Dredge scallops in flour, shaking off excess. Dip each scallop in egg, letting excess drip off, and coat well with coconut. In a 10-inch skillet heat oil over moderate heat until hot but not smoking and cook scallops until golden and just cooked through, about 1½ minutes on each side. Drain scallops on paper towels. Serve scallops with lime wedges.
Makes 4 servings.

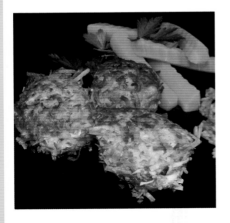

Scallops are low in calories and cholesterol, rich in high-quality protein, a good source of potassium, vitamin B12 and OMEGA-3 fatty acids. Per 100 grams: 88 calories, 33 mg cholesterol, 17 grams protein, 2 grams OMEGA-3.

photo: © Igor Kravtchenko

Coconut Trees at La Sagesse Beach, Grenada, West Indies

Fried Scallop Empanadas (Chile)

Ingredients

Pastry:
3 cups flour (750 g) plus a little more for kneading
1 tsp. salt
1/2 cup (125 ml) cold water
1 egg
1 egg white
1 tsp. vinegar
3 tbsp. shortening

Filling:
24 large scallops
2 onions chopped
1 tbsp. cilantro
3 tbsp. vegetable or olive oil
2 bouillon cubes
oregano and black pepper to taste
1/3 cup (75 ml) table cream
oil for frying

Method

In a bowl, beat the water, egg, egg white and vinegar together. Set aside. In a separate bowl, mix together the flour and salt. Cut the shortening into the flour; mix with a pastry blender or two butter knives. Make a well in the center of the flour mixture and pour the liquid ingredients from the first bowl into the well. Mix the wet and dry ingredients with a fork until it becomes stiff. Turn the dough out onto a lightly floured surface. Knead it just until all the flour is incorporated and the dough is smooth. Wrap the dough in plastic and refrigerate for at least 1 hour, but never more than 24 hours. Roll the dough on a floured surface and cut into circles with round cookie cutters or biscuit cutter. If you don't have cutters, you can use a coffee can or a glass for large or small rounds.

Fry onion in oil, add cilantro, crumbled bouillon cubes, oregano and pepper. Add the scallops and cook until they release their juices then add the cream and cook for a few more minutes. Remove from heat and let cool. On each pastry circle, place filling in the centre, moisten the edges and close, carefully squeezing well and crimping with a fork. Fry in hot oil until golden brown and leave on absorbent paper. Makes 8 servings.

My first taste of Scallop Empanadas in Chile with Diego Errazuriz, Santiago.

Villarrica Volcano from Villarrica Airstrip near Pucon, Chile

Grilled Scallops with Coral Sauce (New Zealand)

Ingredients

6 large scallops, with coral (roe)
drizzle of olive oil
salt and freshly ground black pepper
splash of white wine
6 tbsp. heavy cream
2 shallots, finely sliced
large handful of spinach
a few sprigs of chervil, to garnish

Method

Preheat a griddle pan. Lightly oil and season the scallops with salt and pepper. Add to the hot griddle and cook for 30 seconds on each side. Deglaze the pan with a splash of white wine and pour into a small saucepan. Add cream to the saucepan and cook until reduced to a thicker consistency. Place the coral of the scallops into a food processor. Pour in the reduced cream and season with salt and pepper. Blend to a smooth puree. Sauté the shallots in a little oil until soft. Add the spinach and season with salt and pepper. Remove from the heat as soon as the spinach is wilted. To serve, arrange the scallops around the spinach and shallots. Spoon over the coral sauce and garnish with sprigs of chervil.
Makes 2 servings.

Diver scallops are special and evoke a sense of exclusivity and careful handling. The thought of an individual fisherman, who knows each crevice and rocky ledge in the local waters, diving to the ocean floor and hand-selecting only the choicest scallops makes the diver scallop very appealing on the menu.

Brian Hartz dives off new Zealand's coast.

Piha Beach, New Zealand.

Honey–Sesame Alaskan Scallops

Ingredients

1 pound (500 g) Alaska scallops or large sea scallops
3 tbsp. lime juice
1 tbsp. vegetable oil
1 tbsp. honey
1 tbsp. soy sauce
¼ tsp. ginger
2 tbsp. toasted sesame seeds

Method

Combine lime juice, oil, honey, soy sauce, and ginger. Add scallops and toss to coat. Cover and refrigerate 1 hour, stirring occasionally. Remove scallops from marinade, reserving marinade. Thread scallops evenly on 4 skewers. Place skewers on shallow baking pan that has been sprayed with a non-stick coating. Broil 4 to 6 inches (10-15 cm) from source of heat 2 to 3 minutes. Turn and baste with reserved marinade and continue broiling 2 to 3 minutes or until scallops are opaque throughout. Place sesame seeds on wax paper and roll each broiled scallop skewer over the seeds to evenly coat on all sides.
Makes 4 servings.

If pearls are a girl's best friend, Craig Fancy's passion for scallop pearls are the answer. Buying the most beautiful pearls from the local fishermen, he creates exquisite pieces of jewellery for his stores in Digby and Annapolis Royal, Nova Scotia. His artistic creations can be seen at www.scalloppearl.ca.

Honey-Sesame Alaskan Scallops

Margarita Scallops (Mexico)

Ingredients

¼ cup (60 ml) tequila
1 cup (250 ml) freshly squeezed lime juice
½ cup (125 ml) freshly squeezed lemon juice
½ cup (125 ml) sugar
1 to 2 jalapenos, stemmed, seeded, and coarsely chopped
¾ cup (180 ml) green onion cut into ½ inch (1 cm) pieces
1 cup (250 ml) chopped cilantro leaves
1 tsp. garlic
½ tsp. salt
1 pound (500 g) large sea scallops
1 tbsp. olive oil
1 lime, quartered
3 tsp. minced cilantro

Method

To make the scallops, place all the ingredients, except the scallops and olive oil, in a blender or food processor, and puree. Taste the mixture and add more jalapeno as desired. Transfer the mixture to a mixing bowl and set aside. Rinse the scallops in cold water and pat dry. In a nonstick sauté pan over high heat, heat the olive oil just until smoking. Add the scallops to the sauté pan and sear well without stirring or tossing. Add the citrus mixture to the pan, and bring to a boil. When the liquid reaches a boil, turn the scallops and cook for one minute more. Remove the scallops, cover to keep warm, and reduce the sauce to half of its original volume over high heat. To serve, divide the scallops among the plates. Pour the liquid from the pan directly over the plates. Garnish with the lime wedges and cilantro.
Makes 4 servings.

Tequila, the most important flavour of Margarita Scallops, is made from the Blue Agave or tequila weed. The piquant flavour makes it a natural to accompany scallops with cilantro and lime.

100% DE AGAVE

AÑEJO

40% ALC.

Product of Mexico

Margarita Scallops

New Orleans Style Scallop Cakes for a Party

Ingredients

5 pounds (2 kg) scallops
4 red peppers, finely chopped
4 green peppers, finely chopped
1 cup (250 ml) green onions, finely chopped
1 medium red onion, finely chopped
3 cups (750 ml) breadcrumbs
1 tsp ground white pepper
½ tsp. cayenne pepper
6 eggs
1 cup (250 ml) mayonnaise
2 tbsp. Dijon mustard
4 tbsp. Worcestershire sauce
3 tsp. hot sauce
1 tbsp. fresh coriander
vegetable oil to sauté cakes

Curry- Ginger Sauce

¼ cup (60 ml) olive oil
1 small onion, diced
1 clove garlic, minced
¼ tsp. fresh ginger root, chopped
½ stalk lemongrass, chopped
2½ tbsp. curry powder
¼ tsp. cayenne pepper
2 cups (500 ml) coconut milk
1 cup (250 ml) whipping
 cream (35%)
salt and pepper

Method

Cook the scallops in boiling salted water for about 3 minutes for sea scallops and 1-2 minutes for bay scallops. Reserve the cooking water. Pick the scallop meat into small bits by hand. Mix all dry ingredients together, mix the wet ingredients together and then combine everything. Add enough of the salted water until the mixture is nice and wet. Form them into pucks using about 2 tablespoons of mixture for each. Brown in medium hot oil on both sides and sear until done. Serve with a variety of dipping sauces from sweet to hot (curry-ginger sauce, red pepper coulis, mango chutney* or your favorite seafood sauce.)
Serves all of your friends.

Add onion, garlic, ginger and lemongrass to oil that has been heated in a medium pot over medium-high heat. Sauté for 5 minutes. Reduce the heat to medium. Dust with curry and cayenne pepper and sauté for a few minutes. Deglaze the pot with coconut milk and cream; simmer for 5 minutes. Season to taste and strain through a fine sieve into a small pot. Serve with scallops or other seafood.
Makes approximately 3 cups.

Appetizers

New Orleans Style Scallop Cakes can be served with a variety of dipping sauces

Scallop and Caviar Blini (Russia)

Ingredients

12-15 blini (Use Scallop Crepes recipe page 146)
¼ pound (125 g) scallops
4 ounces (100 g) salmon caviar (or Osetra sturgeon caviar if you can afford it)
sour cream

Method

Prepare blini according to recipe and keep warm. Cook scallops in boiling salted water for 3 – 4 minutes. Allow to cool and chop in fine bits. Place a warm crepe on a flat plate. Spread about 1 teaspoon of sour cream across the middle of the crepe and place a small amount of caviar and scallops on sour cream. Roll the crepe into a small tube and slice into separate bites and enjoy!
Makes 50 – 60 bite-servings.

Moscow lights

Scallop Carpaccio (France)

Ingredients

4 King scallops
4 slim spring onions
2 tbsp. poppy seeds
4 tbsp. good quality olive oil
4 tbsp. fresh lime juice

Method

Clean the scallops and pat the white flesh dry. Cut in thin slices horizontally, about ¼ inch (0.5 cm) thick. Arrange on plates in layers. Wash the spring onions and slice thinly. Scatter over the plates. Toast the poppy seeds in a pan until fragrant, then sprinkle over the scallops in a 1 inch (2 cm) line lengthways. Drizzle with the olive oil and lime juice and serve immediately, with a fresh, crusty baguette to mop up the juices.
Makes 2 servings.

Scallops are actually a very good source of an important nutrient for cardiovascular health, vitamin B12, which is needed by the body to convert homocysteine, a chemical that can damage blood vessel walls, into other benign chemicals. Since high levels of this chemical are associated with an increased risk for atherosclerosis, diabetic heart disease, heart attack, and stroke, it's a good idea to be sure that your diet contains plenty of vitamin B12. Four ounces of scallops contains 33.3% of the daily value for vitamin B12.

Mont Saint-Michel, Normandy, France. photo © Daniel Gallon

Scallop Carpaccio

Scallop Fritters (Caribbean)

Ingredients

2 cups (500 ml) water
1 medium carrot, ground
1 medium onion, ground
dash hot pepper sauce (such as Tabasco)
¾ tbsp. thyme
1 tbsp. garlic powder
1 tbsp. seasoned salt
1 tbsp. black pepper
½ cup (125 ml) sweet pepper (capsicum) ground
4 to 6 cups (1- 1½ l) flour (self-rising)
3 pounds (1½ kg) fresh scallops, ground

Method

Mix the first 6 ingredients. Add enough of the flour to form a thick batter then add the remaining ingredients. Note: The batter should be stiff enough to roll like a meatball. Next roll in flour and drop into oil heated to 350°F (180°C) and cook until brown. Serve with tangy cocktail sauce along with tartar sauce.
Makes 15 servings for cocktail guests.

Small scallops are found almost 310 feet (100 meters) below the water's surface. Scallops often form "beds" on the ocean floor, as deep as almost 1,300 feet (400 meters) below the surface. Survival rates are enhanced in these areas, where currents supply abundant primary production to the bottom.

A floating fishmarket in Willemstad, Curacao

Scallop Sandwiches - Latkes (Israel)

Ingredients

12 large fresh sea scallops
2 cups (500 ml) sunflower or vegetable oil
1 cup (250 ml) chicken broth
¼ cup (75 ml) lemon juice
¼ cup (75 ml) orange juice
4 large potatoes
2 tbsp. olive oil
2 tbsp. flour
1 tbsp. finely chopped chervil
1 tbsp. finely chopped chives
coarse Kosher salt,
freshly ground white pepper

Method

Line a baking sheet with parchment paper. Pour the chicken stock into a saucepan; bring to a boil; reduce to about 2 tablespoons. Cut the scallops in half horizontally; dry on paper towels. Peel, dry and grate the potatoes lengthwise; place in a tea towel and press out the liquid; divide the potatoes into two batches and fluff them up with a fork. Take half the potatoes and form 12 small mounds on the baking sheet; sprinkle each with a little flour. Place two scallop slices on each mound, overlapping slightly; season generously with salt and pepper. Divide the remaining potatoes into 12 portions and place on top of the scallops to form 12 sandwiches; season with salt and pepper and sprinkle with flour. Do not press down.

The sandwiches won't wait, so use 2 large non-stick pans, placing 1 cup (250 ml) oil in each; heat on medium heat for 2 minutes. When the oil is hot, place 6 sandwiches in each pan, using a spatula to ensure they keep their shape. Reduce the heat a little and brown for about 5 minutes. Turn and cook on the other side until nicely browned, transfer to a paper towel-lined cookie sheet and place in a warm oven with the door open while you make the sauce.
Add the lemon and orange juice to the saucepan containing the reduced chicken stock; bring to a boil; boil for 4 minutes or until the sauce has thickened enough to coat the back of a spoon. Whisk in the butter; season with salt and pepper; add the herbs last. Pour a ribbon of sauce around each plate; place 2 sandwiches on top, and serve immediately.
Makes 6 servings.

Jerusalem from Mount Olive

Scallop Tartare (Quebec)

Ingredients

½ pound (250 g) fresh scallops
finely chopped
2 tbsp. dry cranberries finely
chopped
2 tbsp. chives chopped very fine
2 tbsp. grapefruit juice
1 tbsp. olive oil
caviar or lump fish to decorate
(optional)
salt and pepper

Method

Mix all ingredients in a bowl and cool in the refrigerator for approximately 30 minutes. Put in 12 small plates or wonton spoons, decorate with caviar. Serve immediately.
Makes 12 servings.

Waterfront of Quebec City

Scallop Wrapped in Smoked Salmon with Horseradish Mousse

Ingredients

½ pound (250 g) fresh shucked Digby (sea) scallops
½ pound (250 g) smoked salmon
chives and fresh garlic tips
1 cup (250 ml) white wine
1 cup (250 ml) mayonnaise
2 tbsp. red onion minced
2 tbsp. horseradish rinsed and patted dry
2 tbsp. grated unpeeled Cortland apple
2 tsp. Dijon mustard
sugar to taste
1½ tbsp. tarragon cider vinegar

Method

In a sauté pan over low heat add wine, garlic tips and chives. Bring to a bubbling simmer and add scallops, stirring gently until the scallops are opaque and slightly firm to the center. Cool the scallops by placing them directly into a bowl with ice to stop them cooking. Roll gently in ice until scallops are cool.

Cut each piece of smoked salmon into thin long strips and roll the scallop into salmon so that in forms a neat bundle. Mix all ingredients for the mousse and dollop a spoonful onto the serving plate with the wraps. Serve immediately with lemon.

Makes 2 to 4 servings.

Horseradish Mousse

½ cup (125 ml) mayonnaise
1 tbsp. red onion minced
2 tbsp. grated Cortland or other firm, tart apple (peel left on)
1 tbsp. horseradish, rinsed and patted dry
1 tsp. Dijon mustard
sugar to taste
1 tbsp. tarragon cider vinegar

Scallop-Cantaloupe-Foie Gras Tartare (Montreal)

Ingredients

½ pound (200 g) fresh scallops, finely diced
¾ cup (150 g) ripe cantaloupe, finely diced
¼ cup (60 ml) virgin olive oil
2 tbsp. (30 ml) raspberry vinegar
1 tbsp. (15 ml) whipping cream
1 tbsp. (15 ml) violet mustard or other flavoured mustard
1 tbsp. (15 ml) fresh dill, minced (set aside sprigs for garnish)
salt and freshly ground pepper to taste
2 oz. (60 g) foie gras, finely diced
pink peppercorns to garnish

Method

In a bowl, combine all ingredients except foie gras. Gently fold in foie gras so that the dices remain whole. Spoon tartare into two elegant goblets or serving dishes. Garnish with sprigs of dill and pink peppercorns.
Makes 4 servings.

You'll find scallops sold already shucked. Scallops should not be pure white and they should never be stored in water. Pure white scallops most likely have been sitting in and absorbing water or chemicals, losing nutrients and colour. The colour of fresh scallops should range from pale beige to creamy pink, and the meat should have a clean, fresh smell with a moist sheen.

Scallops with a Bourbon Touch (New Orleans)

Ingredients

2 tbsp. bourbon
3 tbsp. green onions, minced
2 tbsp. maple syrup
1 tbsp. low sodium soy sauce
1 tbsp. Dijon mustard
¼ tsp. pepper
24 large sea scallops
6 slices bacon*
dash of Tabasco Sauce

Method

Combine first 6 ingredients in a bowl, stir well and add scallops. Marinate in refrigerator one hour, stirring occasionally. Remove scallops, reserve marinade. Cut each slice of bacon into 4 pieces. Wrap 1 bacon piece around each scallop. Bacon might only wrap halfway around scallops if they are very large. Thread scallops onto 4 skewers, leaving some space so bacon will cook. Place skewers on a broiler pan coated with cooking spray. Broil 8 minutes or until bacon is crisp and scallops are done, basting with reserved marinade.

To ensure that scallops are not overcooked, bacon can be partially cooked in the microwave before assembling or you might use the pre-cooked bacon.
Makes 4 servings.

A popular, simple and quick method of cooking scallops is to roll them in flour and sauté in butter, the way my Mum used to cook them. They can be prepared in about 10 minutes and can be served with any type of vegetables and potatoes or rice. A very popular method, especially at fairs and exhibitions around the east coast of North America is breaded and deep fried. Scallops 'n Chips anyone?

Photo courtesy Nova Scotia Tourism, Culture and Heritage

Louisiana Tabasco Sauce and chillies will give heat to scallop dishes.

Scallops with Sun Dried Tomato Basil Cream Sauce (Virginia)

Chef Greg Hopkins, 19th Street Bistro, Virginia Beach

Ingredients

10 10-20 fresh sea scallops
2 cups heavy cream
½ cup of sun dried tomatoes
5 fresh basil leaves
pinch of kosher salt
2 pinches of seasoning salt
½ cup parmesan cheese
5 cups prepared pasta (we use linguini)
¼ cups toasted pine nuts

Method

Toasted Pine Nuts:
On medium high heat melt two tablespoons of butter then add pine nuts. Keep nuts moving until golden brown.

Sun Dried Tomato Basil Cream Sauce:
In a medium sauce pan start scalding the cream; add the sun dried tomatoes and both salts. Continue to scald and stir the cream so it doesn't boil over or burn. Add the basil and continue reducing. When reduced by half add parmesan cheese. Toss pasta into sauce.

Pan Seared Sea Scallops:
Coat scallops in seasoning salt and peanut oil. Turn sauté pan on high and heat up for 2-3 minutes. Cook scallops for 2-3 minutes on each side for a medium-rare scallop. After scallops are done arrange on pasta and add pine nuts.
Makes 2-4 servings.

Chef Greg was instrumental in making Croc's the first Green Restaurant in Virginia. He worked on the new 'green' menu incorporating local, organic and sustainable ingredients into his dishes.

Chef Greg Hopkins, Croc's 19th Street Bistro, Virginia Beach

Scallops with Basil Cream Sauce

Sea Scallop Tapas with Baguette (Spain)

Ingredients

1½ pound (750 g) sea scallops
¼ cup (50 ml) olive oil
1 4-oz (125 ml) jar diced pimiento, including liquid
2 tbsp. garlic, fresh, finely minced
1 bunch green onions, chopped
2 tbsp. lime juice, fresh
2 tsp. Tabasco Sauce
salt and pepper to taste

Method

In large bowl, toss scallops with olive oil until all scallops are well coated. Place large sauté pan over high heat. When pan is very hot, arrange scallops one layer thick but do not crowd them as they will not caramelize. Sauté for 1½ to 2 minutes. Turn scallops and add remaining ingredients. Toss and continue to sauté for an additional 1½ to 2 minutes over high heat. Serve scallops on individual plates accompanied by baguette slices, or on a large platter allowing your guests to serve themselves.

As an entrée: Deglaze pan with one cup of cream, white wine or stock (chicken, clam or fish) and serve over hot pasta, garnishing with chopped parsley and shredded Manchego cheese.

Makes 8 servings as an appetizer or serves 4 as an entrée.

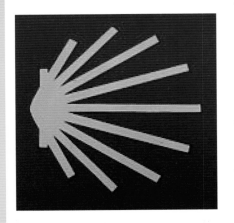

The Camino de Santiago (or Way of St. James) is a 480 km (300 mile) Christian pilgrimage concluding at the cathedral in Santiago de Compostela, Spain. The most popular route stretches from southern France across northern Spain to Santiago. In centuries past, pilgrims would know which houses and hospices along the route would offer shelter and food by the scallop shell outside the door - and pilgrims would wear a scallop shell to be identified as pilgrims. Today, the official symbol is a stylized scallop shell in yellow on a blue background.

Appetizers

Pasajes de San Juan, Guipúzcoa

Spicy Raw Scallop Sushimi

Ingredients

1 jalapeno pepper finely chopped
12 jumbo raw scallops, sliced into
3 discs, about 4 scallops per person
is plenty
juice from 3-4 large limes + zest of
one
1 tbsp. olive oil
salt and pepper
1 avocado
1 tomato, seeded and chopped
½ tsp. cilantro

Method

Combine jalapeno pepper, lime juice and zest, olive oil, pinch of salt and pepper. Completely submerge the scallop slices in the solution for 1 hour, no more. Remove the scallops from the liquid. Prepare a mixture of chopped avocado, tomato, and finely chopped cilantro. Stir in a spoonful or 2 of the liquid from the scallops. Lay the scallops on your choice of serving dish or in martini glasses. Spoon some of the mixture on the scallops and serve cold.
Makes 3 servings.

A lesser-known scallop, the calico scallop (Argopecten gibbus) is caught in very limited quantities in the south-eastern U.S. and is even smaller than the bay scallop. Calico scallop populations have almost collapsed from fishing pressure, however, and dredging for calicos has disrupted extensive amounts of seafloor habitat. Atlantic calicos are sometimes sold as bay scallops so check the label to be sure they are indeed the more numerous bay scallops.

Scallops can be served simply with ginger, Wasabi and Soy Sauce for dipping or with a number of condiments

Welsh Scallop Kiss to warm the cockles of your heart (Wales)

Appetizers

Ingredients

4 ounces (100 g) of bacon
8 scallops
7 ounces (200 g) laverbread*
4 ounces (100 g) cockles (mussels or clams can be substituted)
2 tbsp. oatmeal
pepper
1/3 cup (50 g) cheese optional

Method

Fry the bacon in olive oil and a small bit of Welsh butter until very crisp; remove from pan and keep warm. Combine the laverbread and oatmeal, lightly season (laverbread is fairly salty) then shape into patties and fry in bacon juices. Sear the scallops (you can slice them into two if desired) both sides and place one on top of each laverbread patty. Add the cockles to the pan and heat them through until they slightly 'pop' and become crispy. Assemble the scallop on top of the laverbread patty, drizzle the bacon lardoons over and around the patty and do the same with the cockles. Then drizzle olive oil or melted butter over the top and squeeze a small bit of lemon juice over the top. Grated welsh or mature cheese can be added to the laverbread and oatmeal mixture to make it richer, as can garlic to taste.
Makes 4 servings as a starter or for breakfast.

Laverbread is a traditional Welsh seaweed that is harvested, cleaned, cooked and minced to a paste. It is rich in iron and iodine and is eaten in Wales with bacon, eggs, oatmeal, cockles or toast for a hearty meal.
Photo Courtesy Lorraine King

Fishmonger, Courtesy Lorraine King

Penclawd Twilight, North Gower, Swansea, Wales

photo: © Colin Evans

Your Personal Notes

Salads
and
Soups

Caribbean Grilled Scallop Salad

Ingredients

12 large sea scallops
2 tsp. fish rub, divided
cooking spray
5 slices fresh pineapple
4 cups (1 bag) gourmet salad greens
or mixed salad greens
2 small heads torn Boston lettuce
1/3 cup peeled and diced avocado
2 tbsp. mango chutney
2 tbsp. fresh lime juice
2 tsp. olive oil

Method

Preheat grill to high heat. Pat scallops dry with a paper towel. Sprinkle 1½ tsp. fish rub evenly over scallops. Coat scallops with cooking spray. Place scallops on grill rack; grill 3 minutes on each side or until done. Remove scallops. Add pineapple to grill rack and grill 2 minutes on each side. Remove pineapple from grill and chop. Combine salad greens, lettuce, pineapple, and avocado in a large bowl. Chop large pieces of chutney. Combine chutney, lime juice, olive oil, and remaining ½ teaspoon fish rub in a small bowl. Add dressing to salad, and toss well. Divide salad among 4 bowls. Arrange 3 scallops over each salad.
Makes 4 servings.

Mango Chutney

2 large mangoes, peeled and cubed
2 large tart apples, peeled, cored
and chopped
1 small red onion, chopped
½ medium sweet red bell pepper
(capsicum) chopped
½ cup (125 ml) golden raisins
3 tbsp. grated fresh ginger
1 cup (250 ml) granulated sugar
½ cup (125 ml) white wine vinegar
1 tbsp. lemon juice
½ tsp. each: turmeric, nutmeg powder,
cinnamon, cloves and salt
pepper to taste

Combine all the ingredients except the lemon juice and spices in a heavy stainless steel, glass or enamel saucepan and bring to a boil over high heat. Reduce the heat and simmer uncovered for 20 minutes or until the fruit is tender and the mixture is softened. Stir occasionally. Add the lemon juice and all the spices. Cook for an additional 5 minutes. Remove from the heat and let cool. Pour the chutney into jars, cover and refrigerate for up to 2 weeks.
Makes 2 cups.

St.James's Club, Antigua

Kale, Apple and Scallop Salad (British Columbia)

Pia Carroll and Sinclair Philip, Sooke Harbour House, Vancouver Island

Ingredients

3½ tbsp. blueberry or raspberry vinegar
5 tbsp. oil
1 tsp. Dijon or Meaux mustard
1 tbsp. heavy cream
4 cups (1 l) curly or flat leaf kale, rinsed and torn into bite size pieces
2 Granny Smith Apples cored and cut into 16ths
2 tbsp. unsalted butter
½ pound (250 g) Weathervane scallops, or purple-hinged rock scallops
Nasturtium or chive blossoms

Method

For the vinaigrette, whisk together the vinegar and oil in a small bowl, add the mustard and whisk until the ingredients emulsify and thicken, then add the cream, mix well and reserve. Blanch the kale leaves in boiling water for 15 seconds. Drain and immediately rinse under cold water. Melt 1 tbsp. of the butter in a small frying pan over medium high heat, add the apples and sauté until they are slightly soft and golden, about 5 minutes. Remove apples from the pan and keep warm. Cut the scallops against the grain, into round quarters. Melt the remaining butter in the same pan over medium high heat, add the scallops and sauté until just before they lose their translucence, about 2 minutes. Remove from heat. Arrange the kale leaves on four salad plates. Evenly divide the apple slices among the plates, top with the scallops and pour the vinaigrette over all. Garnish with the nasturtiums or chive blossoms.
Makes 4-6 servings.

Sooke Harbour House
Photo by Qubic Lam

Salads and Soups

Legislative Buildings, Victoria, BC.

Pasta Seafood Salad (Australia)

Ingredients

1 pound (500 g) bay scallop, rinsed
1 pound (500 g) medium raw shrimp, shelled and deveined
½ pound (250 g) small shell pasta (or another interesting shape such as twists)
1 cup (250 ml) tiny frozen peas, thawed
½ cup (125 ml) diced sweet capsicum (red pepper)
½ cup (125 ml) purple onion, finely chopped
½ cup (125 ml) olive oil
½ cup (125 ml) fresh basil leaf
3 tbsp. lemon juice (freshly squeezed)
½ tsp. salt
¼ tsp. pepper
1 cup (250 ml) pitted black olives

Method

Bring a large pot of salted water to boil, drop in the scallops and shrimp, cook for one minute and drain immediately. Bring another large pot of salted water to boil. Cook the pasta as directed on the package, until tender but not mushy. Drain. Toss the cooked pasta and seafood in a large bowl (make sure they are both well drained.) Add the peas (no need to cook them), capiscum and onion, and toss. Place dressing ingredients (olive oil, basil leaves, lemon juice, salt, and pepper) in a food processor bowl fitted with a metal blade. Process until basil is very fine. Pour over the pasta-seafood mixture and blend well. Taste and add salt, pepper, and lemon juice as necessary. Place the salad in a serving bowl or mound it on a platter. Scatter with black olives. Serve immediately, or cover and refrigerate. Salad tastes better when at room temperature, so if refrigerating until later, be sure to take it out of the fridge for 30 minutes before serving.
Makes 6-8 servings.

Scallops are on the list of The World's 100 Healthy Foods along with 5 other fish and seafood species. Foods that make this list must be nutrient-dense, whole, familiar, healthy, readily available, affordable and they have to taste good.

The beach at Byron Bay, Australia

Pomelo and Scallop Salad (Thailand)

Ingredients

vegetable oil for frying
1 tbsp. thinly sliced garlic
2 tbsp. sliced shallots,
½ pound (250 g) scallops
1 large pomelo or 2 sweet grapefruits
2 tsp. roasted chilli paste (optional)
2 tbsp. fresh lime juice
1 tbsp. fish sauce
2 tsp. sugar
1 red jalapeno chilli pepper, seeded
and thinly sliced
1 tbsp. chopped fresh mint
2 tbsp. roasted peanuts, crushed
¼ cup (7 g) fresh cilantro
(coriander) leaves

Method

In a small frying pan, over medium heat, cook garlic and shallots until a light golden brown. Remove, drain and allow to cool. Bring a large saucepan ¾ full of salted water to a boil. Add scallops and cook for 2 minutes. Drain and set aside to cool. Peel the pomelo, divide it into segments and remove the membrane from each segment. Carefully break each segment in smaller pieces. Place them in a bowl. If using grapefruits, treat them in the same way but place the pieces in a sieve to drain.

In a large bowl, combine the roasted chilli paste, lime juice, fish sauce, sugar and jalapeno pepper. Stir until the sugar dissolves. Add the scallops, pomelo or grapefruit, mint, fried shallots, fried garlic and peanuts and toss to mix. Turn out onto a serving plate, garnish with cilantro and serve.

Makes 4 – 6 servings.

photo: © Tourism Authority of Thailand

Festival in Thailand

Scallop Salad (New Zealand)

Ingredients

1½ pounds (750 g) scallops
2 tbsp. olive oil
1 garlic clove
juice of 1 lemon
½ cup oil
1 clove garlic, crushed
1 tsp. ginger, fresh, grated
1 tbsp. sesame oil
lettuce
1 capiscum (red pepper) julienned
fresh whole cilantro
12 mushrooms

Method

Mix dressing ingredients (lemon juice, ½ cup olive oil, garlic, ginger and sesame oil) and put aside while preparing the rest of the dish. On each plate arrange a bed of lettuce, mushrooms on either end with heads pointing out, sprinkle capiscum from center out (like spokes of a wheel) and arrange whole cilantro amongst the peppers. Sauté the scallops in the olive oil and garlic until golden brown but just done. Drain and then pile in the middle of each plate. Pour dressing over top and serve immediately.
Makes 6 servings.

Scallops have between sixty and one hundred eyes that seem to glow in the water. When a shadow is cast over a bed of scallops, they will swim awkwardly away by flapping their two shells together, expelling water as their propulsion. To some divers this looks hilarious, as they say the scallops look like sets of false teeth jouncing around.

Scallop showing its many eyes. Courtesy© Bob Semple.

Scallop Salad

Scallops, Green Beans and Horseradish Salad (Brazil)

Ingredients

2 pounds (1 kg) fresh or frozen fine green beans
1 pound (500 g) bay or sea scallops
2 tbsp. creamed horseradish
2 tbsp. sour cream
4 tbsp. mayonnaise
3 shallots, finely chopped
2 garlic clove, crushed
2 - 3 dashes of Worcestershire sauce
salt and fresh ground black pepper
2 hard-boiled eggs, peeled and grated
6 rashers bacon, finely chopped

Method

Bring 2 saucepans of salted water to the boil. To one, add the beans and blanch for 2 minutes. Drain, plunge into ice-water, then drain and set aside. To the other pot, add the scallops. Cook for 2 minutes, drain and set aside on paper towels. If using sea scallops, cut in smaller pieces. Using a small bowl, whisk together the horseradish, sour cream, mayonnaise, shallots and garlic. Season with Worcestershire sauce, salt and freshly ground pepper. Toss the drained beans with the horseradish dressing. Gently mix in the scallops. Plate and top with fresh ground pepper.
Makes 8 servings.

Most restaurants receive their scallops opened and packed but some prefer to buy them from the fishermen live and in the shell. Live scallops, which are eaten whole like clams or oysters, are also increasingly popular.

Photo by Patrick McMurray

Scallops, Green Beans and Horseradish Salad

Scallops, Spinach, Shiitake Salad with Truffle Emulsion (Ottawa)

Executive Chef Michael Blackie, Ottawa

Ingredients

3 tbsp. champagne vinegar
¼ cup (60 ml) olive oil (first pressed)
4 tbsp. soya sauce
1 tbsp. truffle oil
1 tsp. chopped fresh thyme
salt and pepper to taste
12 shiitake mushrooms, medium sized
2 medium shallots, chopped
4 tsp. olive oil
3 cups (750 ml) baby spinach leaves
salt and pepper to taste
12 large sea scallops (10 per pound)
3 tbsp. cubed unsalted butter
3 tbsp. vegetable oil
salt and white pepper to taste

Method

Place all ingredients except oil in mixing bowl. Slowly whisk in oil in a thin line.

Preheat oven to 375ºF (180ºC). Clean mushrooms by removing stem completely. Toss mushrooms and shallots in oil; season to taste. Roast in oven for 10 to 15 minutes until soft, turning a few times. Wash spinach leaves and set aside for later. When mushrooms are finished take out and let cool to room temperature; slice into strips and reserve in their natural juices.

Preheat sauté pan on medium to high with oil. Season the scallops with salt and pepper and place in hot pan. Cook the scallops for approximately 4 minutes on one side, (Hint: do not touch them as you want them to caramelize; if they are sticking do not worry as halfway through the cooking process they will start to come free.) After two minutes, add butter to the pan (this will help to promote colour and flavour.) In the last 30 seconds turn over the scallops and finish the pan off with approximately 3 tbsp. of the dressing. Immediately remove the scallops from the pan and reserve for plating. Mix mushrooms and baby spinach leaves together with some of the emulsion and place in the center of the plate. Place hot scallops around salad. Gently spoon a small amount of soya truffle emulsion on each scallop and served immediately.
Makes 4 servings.

Chef Michael Blackie, Brookstreet Hotel and National Arts Centre

photo Courtesy Ottawa Tourism

Rideau Canal Skateway with National Arts Centre and Parliament Hill.

Sweet Potato and Scallop Soup with Coconut (Caribbean)

Ingredients

2 pounds (1 kg) sweet potatoes, peeled and cut into chunks
½ cup (125 ml) butter
1 onion, peeled and sliced
2 carrots, peeled and sliced
½ cup (125 ml) chopped garlic
½ cup (125 ml) chopped peeled fresh ginger
1 or 2 jalapeno peppers, sliced, with seeds (to taste)
2 tbsp. curry powder
1 large tart apple, peeled and diced
4 cups (1 l) low- or no-sodium chicken broth
1-14 oz. can (450 ml) unsweetened coconut milk
salt and freshly ground pepper and cider vinegar, to taste
½ pound (250 g) bay scallops
zest of 1 orange
¼ cup (60 ml) chopped fresh cilantro leaves
¼ cup (60 ml) raisins
2 tbsp. mango chutney
½ cup (125 ml) heavy cream whipped until soft peaks form
½ cup (125 ml) unsweetened shredded coconut, light toasted

Method

Toss sweet potatoes in 2 tablespoons melted butter; cover and bake in 400ºF (200ºC) oven for 30 minutes. In a large heavy pan, heat half of the butter over medium heat. Add onion and carrots, cover and cook for 15 minutes, stirring occasionally, until vegetables are softened. Add garlic, ginger, jalapenos and curry; cook for 1 minute and then stir in roasted sweet potatoes and apple. Add broth, bring to a boil and reduce to a simmer. Cook, uncovered, for 20 to 30 minutes, or until vegetables are very tender. Let cool. In a blender or food processor, puree soup in batches or use a hand beater to puree in the pot. Whisk in coconut milk. Soup may be prepared ahead to this point. Re-warm soup over low heat, stirring. Season to taste with salt, pepper and cider vinegar. In a heavy skillet, sauté scallops in remaining butter. Add orange zest, scallops, cilantro and raisins to soup. Keep warm. Fold mango chutney into whipped cream and reserve. Ladle soup into serving bowls and spoon a dollop of mango chutney-whipped cream in centre of each. Sprinkle with toasted coconut, if desired. Serve immediately.
Makes 8 servings.

St.George's, Grenada

Light Creamy Scallop Chowder with Salsify (Netherlands)

Ingredients

juice of 1 lemon
¾ pound (375 g) salsify (also called Jerusalem artichokes and sunchokes)
¼ pound (125 g) sliced bacon, cut crosswise into strips
1 large white onion, finely chopped
kosher salt and freshly ground black pepper
½ cup (125 ml) dry white wine
2 cups (500 ml) clam juice
1 cup (250 ml) water
4 thyme sprigs
1 cup (250 ml) whipping cream (35%)
2 pounds (1 kg) bay scallops
pinch of cayenne pepper
1 tbsp. chopped parsley

Method

Fill a medium bowl with cold water and add the lemon juice. Peel and dice the salsify and add to the lemon water. In a large saucepan, cook the bacon over moderate heat until crisp, about 5 minutes. With a slotted spoon, transfer the bacon to paper towels to drain; reserve 2 tablespoons of the bacon fat in the saucepan. Add the onion to the saucepan and cook over moderate heat until softened, about 5 minutes. Drain the salsify. Add it to the saucepan and season with salt and black pepper. Cover and cook over moderately low heat, stirring occasionally, until the salsify is almost tender, about 10 minutes. Add the wine to the saucepan and bring to a boil. Add one-half of the clam juice, water and thyme. Cover and simmer over moderately low heat until the salsify is tender, about 10 minutes longer. Add the cream, scallops, remainder of clam juice and cayenne pepper and simmer for 5 minutes, or until the scallops are just cooked through. Discard the thyme sprigs. Season the chowder with salt and black pepper and ladle into warmed bowls. Top with the bacon and parsley and serve.
 Makes 4-6 servings.

Scallops are categorized by size, the smaller the number, the larger the scallop; the number represents the number of scallops to a pound. For example, you would need about fifteen grade 10-20 scallops to make a pound but you would need a significant amount more of grade 80-100 scallops to make a pound.

Salads and Soups

Leiden Windmill, Netherlands

Potato Bacon Scallop Chowder (Newfoundland)

Ingredients

1 pound (500 g) small sea scallops
2 large potatoes peeled and cubed
1 cup (250 ml) water
8 bacon strips
1 cup (250 ml) chopped onion
½ cup (125 ml) chopped celery
1-10 oz. (300 ml) can condensed cream of chicken soup, undiluted
1¾ cups (325ml) milk
1 cup (250 ml) sour cream
½ tsp. salt
dash pepper
1 tbsp. minced fresh parsley

Method

In a large saucepan, cover and cook potatoes in water until tender. Meanwhile, in a large skillet, cook bacon until crisp; remove to paper towels to drain and set aside. In the same skillet, sauté onion and celery in drippings until tender; drain. Add to undrained potatoes. Stir in scallops, soup, milk, sour cream, salt and pepper. Cook over low heat for 10 minutes or until heated through, but do not boil. Crumble bacon; set aside ¼ cup to be sprinkled on the soup along with parsley.
Makes 6 servings.

Sea scallops have a somewhat uncommon combination of life-history attributes: low mobility, rapid growth and low natural mortality. These attributes enable sea scallop populations to respond rapidly after areas have been closed to fishing. The largest single fishery for sea scallops is in the northeast Atlantic from Canada to Virginia and most sea scallops consumed in the US are caught by Canadian fishermen.

Cape Spear Lighthouse, St. John's Newfoundland

Scallop Bisque (Maine)

Ingredients

2-10 oz. cans (600 ml) condensed cream of mushroom soup, undiluted
1-10 oz. can (300 ml) condensed cream of celery soup, undiluted
2¾ cups (750 ml) milk
4 green onions, chopped
½ cup (125 ml) chopped celery
1 garlic clove, minced
1 tsp. Worcestershire sauce
¼ tsp. hot pepper sauce
2 pounds (1 kg) uncooked medium scallops, rinsed in cool water
½ cup (125 ml) canned whole mushrooms, drained
3 tbsp. Madeira wine or chicken broth
½ tsp salt
½ tsp. pepper
minced fresh parsley

Method

In a Dutch oven or soup kettle, combine the first eight ingredients. Mix well and bring to a boil. Reduce heat; add scallops and mushrooms. Simmer, uncovered, for 5 minutes. Stir in the wine or broth, salt and pepper; cook 2-3 minutes longer. Garnish with parsley.
Makes 10 servings.

Scallops are sweet, tender, clean, available year-round and virtually all-purpose. There really is no reason to play around with the distinct and subtle flavour of scallops. A good chef can emphasize their sweetness, saltiness and texture but above all, the essence must be preserved.

Scallop Bisque

Scallop Chowder Down-Home Style (Nova Scotia)

Ingredients

2 large leeks (white and pale green parts only)washed and finely chopped
1 tbsp. unsalted butter
1 large russet (baking) potato
2 tbsp. dry white wine
1 fresh thyme sprig
white pepper
¾ pound (375 g) bay scallops
3½ cups (1 l) bottled clam juice
1 medium carrot, diced
1 large celery rib, diced
2 slices bacon, chopped
½ cup (125 ml) whole milk
salt and pepper to taste

Method

Wash leeks well in a bowl of cold water, then drain well. Cook half of leeks in butter in a large heavy saucepan over low heat, covered, stirring occasionally, until very soft, about 10 minutes. While leeks are cooking, peel and dice potato. Add wine, thyme, and white pepper to leeks and boil until most of liquid is evaporated, about 1 minute. Add ½ of the diced potato, (reserve the rest in a bowl of cold water) ¼ of the scallops, and clam juice, then simmer, uncovered, until potato is tender, about 15 minutes.

Drain remaining potatoes in a colander and cook with carrot, celery, and remaining leeks in a medium size saucepan of boiling salted water until just tender, about 5 minutes, then drain. Cook bacon in a skillet over moderate heat, stirring occasionally, until crisp, about 3 minutes, and transfer to paper towels to drain. Remove and discard thyme sprig. Puree soup in 2 batches in a blender or with a hand blender until very smooth (use caution when blending hot liquids) and transfer to a bowl. Return soup to cleaned saucepan, then add vegetable mixture, remaining scallops, milk and salt and cook over moderate heat (do not boil), stirring, until scallops are just cooked through, about 2 minutes. Sprinkle with bacon and serve with herbed crackers.

Makes 4 main-course servings.

Nova Scotia Harbour

Scallop Soup (Tunisia)

Ingredients

1½ pounds (750 g) scallops, chopped
2 small onions
1 garlic clove
2 tbsp. tomato puree
1 tbsp. paprika
½ tsp. cayenne pepper
½ tsp. cumin
6 cups (1.5 l) water
½ cup (100 g) pearl barley
juice of 1 lemon
2 tbsp. chopped parsley
6 tbsp. olive oil
salt

Method

Wash scallops in cold water to remove any grit and chop in small pieces. Peel and finely chop the onion and garlic. Heat oil in large pan and fry onion until transparent. Add the garlic, tomato puree, paprika, cayenne, cumin and a little salt. Stir fry for 2 – 3 minutes. Add water and bring to a boil. Lower the heat and leave to cook 5 minutes. Add the pearl barley and cook for 20 – 30 minutes, covered. Add the chopped scallop meat and simmer for 10 minutes. Ladle into soup bowls, sprinkle lemon juice and serve.
Makes 4 servings.

Stop cooking scallops when the outer surface of the scallop turns solidly opaque but the centre is not fully cooked. They're great to sauté, but take care not to overcrowd the pan. Cook in small batches or they will poach rather than sauté.

Colourful ingredients for Scallop Soup

Spicy Scallop Bisque (San Francisco, California)

Ingredients

1 pound (500 g) sea scallops cut in small pieces or small bay scallops
1 medium onion
1 celery rib
1 carrot
1 vine-ripened tomato
1 head garlic (not 1 clove of garlic)
2 tbsp. olive oil
2 tbsp. chipotle peppers, chopped
2 tbsp. chopped fresh tarragon leaves
2 tbsp. chopped fresh thyme leaves
1 bay leaf
8 black peppercorns
2 cups (500 ml) vegetable or chicken broth
½ cup (125 ml) brandy
½ cup (125 ml) dry sherry
4 cups (1 l) fish stock
¼ cup (75 ml) tomato paste
½ cup (125 ml) heavy cream
1½ tbsp. cornstarch
2 tbsp. water

Method

Chop onion, celery, carrot, and tomato. Halve garlic head crosswise and roast in oven or on barbecue and remove flesh. In a large heavy pot, heat oil over moderately high heat until hot but not smoking. Add vegetables, garlic, herbs, peppercorns, brandy, and sherry and simmer, stirring, until almost all liquid is evaporated, about 5 minutes. Add vegetable broth and fish stock. Simmer mixture, uncovered, stirring occasionally, 1 hour. Pour mixture through a fine sieve into a large saucepan, pressing on and discarding solids. Whisk in tomato paste and simmer until reduced to about 3 cups (750 ml,) about 10 minutes. Add cream and chipotle peppers and simmer bisque 5 minutes. In a small bowl stir together cornstarch and water and whisk into bisque. Simmer for 2 minutes, stirring and allowing bisque to thicken slightly. Add chopped scallops and simmer bisque 1 minute, or until scallops are just cooked through. Season with salt and pepper and garnish with chives or paprika.
Makes 4 to 6 servings.

Andy Peay had just established a winery in the hills of Sonoma, California and was in the process of planting Pinot Noir grapes. A few feet into the soil he came upon a layer of scallop shells. That would have not been unusual except that his new vineyard was 260 meters (800 feet) above sea level and about 6.5 km (4 miles) from the sea. Geologists point out that during the Pliocene Age, between 2.5 and 5.5 million years ago, the seabed lifted and formed the now famous wine area of Sonoma. Besides the fact that it proves that scallops have been with us for many millions of years, it should not come as a surprise to learn that the "scallopy" soils of the Peary Vineyards in Sonoma produce some of the best Pinot Noir wines in the area. "Our subsoils are littered with the fossils of sea creatures, especially the elegant fan-shaped scallop shell," remarks Andy Peay.

Peay Vineyards, Sonoma, California

Tomato-Rice Soup with Scallops (Washington State)

Ingredients

10 cups (2.5 l) chopped ripe tomatoes
1 tbsp. unsalted butter
1 large onion, chopped
1 small celery stalk, chopped
2 small carrots, peeled and shredded
6 cups (1.5 l) low sodium chicken stock
2 tbsp. cilantro, chopped
2 tbsp. green onions, chopped
4 tbsp. long grain rice
salt and pepper, to taste
1 pound (500 g) fresh scallops
½ cup (125 ml) dry white wine
1 bay leaf

Method

Heat butter in a large saucepan and add onions, celery, and carrots with 1 cup of the chicken stock. Cover and simmer for 10 minutes on low heat, stirring occasionally. Stir in tomatoes and all of the stock except reserve ½ cup of the stock and set aside. Cover and simmer over low heat for an additional 15 minutes, stirring occasionally. When tomatoes are soft, puree soup in a food processor and return to saucepan. Add cilantro, green onions, and rice. Sprinkle with salt and pepper to taste. Simmer, uncovered for 10 minutes or until rice is cooked through or 'al dente'. In a small saucepan, add scallops, wine, bay leaf and reserved chicken stock and bring to a rapid simmer on medium high heat. Turn heat to low and cook until scallops are tender and cooked through. Remove bay leaf and pour scallop mixture into tomato-rice soup mixture and serve.
 Makes 6 servings.

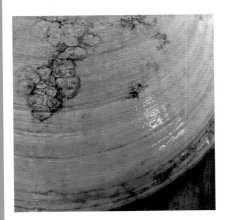

Also known as Smooth or Giant Scallop, the Sea Scallop (Placopecten magelanicus) can live more than 20 years. The age of the scallop can be told by the annuli, the concentric rings of their shells.

Tomato-Rice Soup with Scallop

Scallop-Yam Chowder (Massachusetts)

Ingredients

3 tbsp. bacon drippings
1 lb. (500 g) fresh or frozen sea scallops
1 medium onion, chopped
3 stalks celery, sliced in chunks
1 qt. (1 l) boiling water
¼ cup (125 ml) chopped green pepper
6 medium yams, peeled and sliced in 1-inch (2 cm) pieces
2 cups (500 ml) chicken stock
2 tsp. salt
¼ tsp. pepper
1 cup (250 ml) light cream

Method

Defrost scallops, if frozen and cut in halves. Heat bacon drippings; add onion and celery. Cook over low heat until onion is tender. Add boiling water, green pepper, yams, chicken stock, salt and pepper. Cook over medium heat about 15 minutes. Add scallops; cook 10 to 15 minutes longer, or until yams are tender. Add light cream; heat to serving temperature but do not boil.
Makes 6 servings.

Off Alaska, fishermen dredge for the weathervane scallop (Patinopecten caurinus) a sea scallop with annual catches of about 2,200 to 4,500 MT (five to ten million pounds).

Salads and Soups

Scallop-Yam Chowder

Your Personal Notes

Entrees &
Main Dishes

Baked Scallop Casserole

Ingredients

1 pound (500 g) sea scallops
1 tsp. salt
¼ cup (75 ml) chopped onion
1 cup (250 ml) diced celery
½ cup (125 ml) pimiento
1 can sliced mushrooms, drained
1 cup (250 ml) chopped green pepper
6 tbsp. butter
¼ cup (75 ml) flour
2 cups (500 ml) milk
1 cup (250 ml) soft bread crumbs
1 tbsp. melted butter
¼ cup (75 ml) finely grated parmesan cheese
1 tsp. salt

Method

Separate and rinse scallops. Dry on paper towel and sprinkle with salt. Cook onion, celery, mushrooms and green pepper in 2 teaspoons butter until tender. Make a cream sauce with remaining 4 teaspoons butter, flour, salt and milk. Combine scallops, sautéed vegetables and cream sauce. Place in 1½ quart (2 l) casserole dish. Combine bread crumbs, butter and cheese and sprinkle over top. Bake at 375 °F (180 °C) for approximately 25 minutes.
Makes 6 servings.

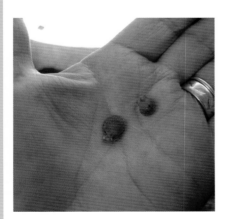

The so-called China Bay Scallop originally came from the U.S. in 1983. A shipment of New England Bay Scallops was sent to China where 26 animals successfully spawned. From that small beginning, the Chinese now farm-raise upwards of 200,000 tons of bay scallops a year in Northeastern China, much of which is exported to the U.S

Baked Scallop Casserole

Bayou Sea Scallops on Angel Hair Pasta (North Carolina)

Chef Lee, Penguin Isle Restaurant, Nags Head

Ingredients

2 tbsp. olive oil
8 large scallops, remove foot (size: 1 oz. per scallop)
3 tbsp. Bayou spice
2 tomatoes, roughly chopped, seedless, skinless
½ cup (125 ml) scallions, chopped
3 tbsp. butter
½ cup (125 ml) beer
4 servings of cooked angel hair pasta

Bayou Spice:
½ tbsp. salt
2 tbsp. granulated garlic
2 tbsp. granulated onion
2 tbsp. dried leaf thyme
2 tbsp. dried leaf oregano
2 tbsp. cayenne pepper
½ tsp. white pepper
2 tsp. paprika
¾ tsp. dried rosemary

Makes than more enough spice for 1 recipe

Method

SPICY! Very tasty - measure Bayou spice accurately - no extra needed

Heat olive oil to medium heat. Toss scallops in Bayou spice. Sauté scallops until half-way done, 1-2 minutes. (Size of scallops determines cooking times.) Add tomatoes and scallions, toss for 20 seconds then add beer and butter and let foam. Reduce until scallops are cooked to a hot medium-rare. Pour over cooked pasta and serve.
Makes 4 servings.

Chef Lee has been serving scallops for twenty years at Penguin Isle Restaurant. He says that for excellent tasting scallop dishes, you must begin with the best and freshest scallops from the Atlantic.

Photo by Three Dog Ink. LLC

Cape Hatteras Lighthouse, Outer Banks, North Carolina, has helped fishermen for over 100 years...

Breaded Scallops (Ireland)

Ingredients

32 King scallops
salt and pepper
flour, for dredging
1 large egg, lightly beaten
1 cup (250 ml) bread crumbs
oil, for deep frying
lemon wedges, garnish

Method

Cut jumbo scallops in half but if using medium scallops, leave whole. Lightly season scallops with salt and pepper. Roll scallops in flour and coat with egg, then roll them in breadcrumbs. Deep fry breaded scallops 2 to 3 minutes. Garnish with lemon and a sprig of parsley and serve with salad and French fries or other potatoes. Makes 4 servings.

Scallop fishing is a deep-rooted tradition, which in Ireland apparently extends back to at least the 16th century. Wild scallops are commercially fished in numerous locations in Ireland and are landed into more than 40 ports around the coast. The modern-day fishery off the southeast coast began in inshore waters, south of the Wexford coast, in the 1970s and gradually expanded offshore and into the south Irish Sea.

Renvyle Castle, County Galway, Ireland.

Breaded Scallops

Bloody Mary Scallops Italian – Virginia

Pamela Barefoot, Blue Crab Co. Malfa

Ingredients

¼ cup olive oil
1 onion, diced
1 green pepper, diced
1 garlic clove, minced
2 cups (500 ml) tomatoes, chopped and drained
½ cup Bloody Mary Mixer (Blue Crab Bay or other brand in your area)
1 pound (500 g) scallops
1 tbsp. butter
¼ cup dry white wine1 tbsp. lemon juice
Italian (spiced) breadcrumbs

Method

Preheat oven to 375°F (190°C). Saute onion, green pepper and garlic in olive oil until tender. Add tomatoes and Bloody Mary mixer. Simmer 15 minutes, stirring occasionally. Meanwhile, sauté scallops for 2-3 minutes in butter. Add wine and lemon juice and simmer 5 minutes. Combine all ingredients in lightly greased baking dish. Sprinkle breadcrumbs on top and bake 5 – 10 minutes until lightly browned. Sprinkle with crumbled feta cheese or grated Parmesan.
Makes 2 – 4 servings.

Pam Barefoot built a company that put the tastes of the Chesapeake region on the map. Pam is a protector of the environment and provides stimulating and fun employment for citizens of her rural community. Scallops are among the foods she like to prepare.

The Chesapecten jeffersonius from Chesapeake Bay, the largest estuary in the world, was the first fossil from North America to be illustrated in a scientific publication. They were so common in this area in the late 1800s that local inhabitants used them in building foundations and as dishes and water ladles. Although this species died out about 4 million years ago, scallops are an important fishery in the area and the Chesapecten jeffersonius is Virginia's state fossil.

Williamsburg, Virginia

Broccoli and Mushroom Scallops

Ingredients

1 pound (500 g) medium sea scallops, sliced in half
1½ cups (400 g) sliced mushrooms
2 tbsp. margarine or butter
1 medium bunch broccoli cut in small chunks
2 oz. (50 g) sliced pimientos
1 can condensed chicken broth
3 tbsp. cornstarch
2 tsp. soy sauce
cooked rice or pasta

Method

In a 3 quart (3 l) saucepan, cook and stir mushrooms in margarine over medium heat until tender, about 5 minutes. Stir in scallops, broccoli, and pimientos. Cook, stirring frequently, for 3 to 4 minutes until scallops start to turn white. Gradually stir chicken broth into cornstarch until smooth. Stir broth mixture and soy sauce into scallop mixture. Heat to boiling, stirring constantly. Reduce heat, simmer and stir 1 minute. Serve over rice.
Makes 2 servings.

Probably the most famous scallop dish is Coquille St.-Jacques. The word coquille means shell in French. This dish has some religious history, but only with regard to the shell itself. The scallop shell was used as a badge of reverence and identification by pilgrims visiting the Spanish shrine of St. James.

Broccoli and Mushroom Scallops

Broiled Scallops in the Shell

Ingredients

2 pounds (1 kg) scallops
½ cup (125 ml) dry vermouth
½ cup (125 ml) olive oil
1 tsp. freshly chopped garlic
½ tsp. salt
2 tbsp. minced parsley

Method

Marinate all ingredients in fridge for 1 hour or more. Place scallops in shallow, rectangular baking pan leaving space between each scallop. Place under broiler for up to five minutes, turning once. Bring marinade to a boil. Serve scallops in scallop shells with heated marinade and garnish with fresh parsley.
Makes 8 servings.

King Scallops are from the waters around the Isle of Man, England, Ireland, Scotland and Wales. The shells range from $4^{1/4}$ - $5^{1/2}$ in. (11 - 14 cm.) wide and have various colours and natural staining on the outside and mainly white on the inside. It is illegal to catch and land scallops smaller than 11 cm wide.

Broiled Scallops in the Shell

Chicken and Scallops Fettuccini (Nova Scotia)

Ingredients

2 tbsp. extra virgin olive oil
½ pound (500 g) bay scallops
2 chicken breasts, boneless and skinless
2 tbsp. oil packed sun-dried tomatoes, chopped
2 tbsp. sun-dried cranberries
1 tbsp. pesto
1 tsp. green peppercorns
2 tbsp. diced apple
2 tbsp. vodka
2 tbsp. white wine
¾ cup (175 ml) whipping cream
6 oz. (200 g) fettuccini, cooked al dente
salt and freshly ground pepper to taste
grated parmesan cheese, as garnish
chopped parsley, as garnish

Method

Heat oil in a large sauté pan over medium-high heat. Slice chicken into bite-sized pieces. Add scallops, chicken, tomatoes, cranberries, pesto, diced apple and green peppercorns. Sauté quickly for 1 minute. Season with salt and pepper and flambé with vodka, then stir in white wine. Add cream and toss with warm pasta. Simmer until cream reduces enough to lightly coat the pasta noodles. Divide between 2 serving plates and sprinkle with parmesan cheese and parsley.
Makes 2 servings.

Scallops are one of the most delectable foodstuffs to come from the sea. Not much more expensive than other bi-valve mollusc cousins, they are so rich, sweet and tender that a little goes a long way.

Ocean View at Chester, Nova Scotia

Chinese Scallop Stir Fry

Ingredients

2 tbsp. vegetable oil
1 pound (500 g) bay scallops, rinsed and dried
2 cups (500 ml) sliced fresh mushrooms
1 8-ounce (250 ml) can sliced water chestnuts, drained
1 red or green pepper, cut into strips
1/3 cup thinly sliced green onions
½ cup (125 ml) chicken broth
3 tbsp. dry sherry
3 tbsp. soy sauce
1 tbsp. cornstarch
½ tbsp. ground ginger
¼ tsp. ground black pepper
1 small package frozen snow peas
3 cups (750 ml) hot cooked rice

Method

Heat oil in wok or large skillet over medium high heat. Add scallops and stir fry 2 minutes. Stir in mushrooms, water chestnuts, pepper, carrot, and onions; stir fry 2 minutes. Combine broth, sherry, soy sauce, cornstarch, ginger, and pepper. Add to wok along with snow peas. Cook 1 to 2 minutes, or until sauce is clear and thickened, stirring frequently. Serve over hot rice.
Makes 6 servings.

Scallops grown in suspension systems or in baskets take six months to three years to reach market size, depending on the final product - whereas bottom grown scallops require a further two to three years.

Guilin, China

Concha de Vieiras - Scallops in a Shell (Spain)

Marimar Torres Winery, California

Ingredients

3 tbsp. butter
6 large garlic cloves, minced
3 large onions, thinly sliced
1 cup (250 ml) dry white wine
½ tsp. salt
½ tsp. freshly ground pepper
2 pounds (1 kg) large sea scallops
2 tbsp. sherry wine vinegar
3-4 tbsp. fine commercial bread crumbs
2 tbsp. olive oil
2 tbsp. chopped parsley

Method

Heat butter in a skillet. Sauté garlic and onions over low heat for about 20 minutes, until soft and golden. Add wine, increase heat to medium and cook for 10 minutes or until wine is almost evaporated. Stir in salt and pepper and arrange as a bed on 6-8 individual scallop shells. Toss scallops with vinegar and marinate for 15 minutes. Distribute scallops on top of onions; sprinkle with bread crumbs, olive oil and parsley. Place under broiler for 4-5 minutes or until scallops are done and breadcrumbs are golden. Serve at once.
Makes 6 to 8 servings.

Marimar Torres, born in Catalonia, Spain, has been involved in wine and food all her life. She lives in San Francisco and oversees the Torres Estate Winery and the two vineyards in Sonoma. Marimar is the author of many cookbooks; this recipe is from The Spanish Table.

Alcala del Jucar (La Mancha), Spain

Coquilles Saint-Jacques with Duchesse Potatoes (France)

Ingredients

Method

1 tsp. lemon juice
½ tsp. salt, dash pepper
2 pounds (1 kg) sea scallops, washed and drained
4 tbsp. butter or margarine
¼ cup (75 ml) finely chopped onion
¼ pound (100g) sliced mushrooms
1/3 cup (50 ml) flour
1 cup (250 ml) light cream
½ cup (125 ml) milk
1 cup (250 ml) grated Gruyere cheese
½ cup (125 ml) dry white wine
1 tbsp. lemon juice
1 tbsp. chopped parsley

Duchesse potatoes

1 lb. (500 g) peeled white potatoes
1 egg
2 tbsp. (30g) unsalted butter
salt and white pepper

In medium saucepan, combine 1 cup water, 1 teaspoon lemon juice and salt and bring to boil. Add scallops; simmer covered for 6 minutes or until tender. Drain on paper towels. Sauté onion and mushrooms until tender in 4 tablespoons hot butter or margarine in saucepan. Remove from heat. Stir in flour and dash of pepper until well blended. Gradually stir in cream and milk. Bring to boil.

Reduce heat and simmer, stirring frequently, 4-5 minutes or until quite thick. Add cheese and stir until melted. Remove from heat and carefully stir in wine, lemon juice and parsley. Add scallops and mix well. Turn into scallop shells or a 1½ quart casserole.

Prepare the Duchesse potatoes (mashed potatoes mixed with the raw egg and seasoned with salt and pepper.) Pipe the potatoes on the filled shells or dish and sprinkle lightly with grated Parmesan cheese. Bake at 400°F (200°C) until lightly coloured and sauce is bubbling.

Makes 8 servings.

Dry and wet scallops: To test if you have indeed purchased dry scallops, toss one in a smoking hot skillet. If it sticks, it's dry. Dry scallops will also have a nutty, brown color, while soaked scallops will be white.

Coquille Saint Jacques

Curried Scallop Cakes (Japan)

Ingredients

1½ pounds (1 kg) fresh sea scallops, chopped in small pieces
¾ cup (175 ml) mayonnaise
3 large egg yolks
3 green onions, chopped
1/3 cup (75 ml) chopped fresh cilantro
1½ tbsp. dry mustard
1½ tbsp. curry powder
¾ tsp. salt
½ tsp. ground black pepper
3 cups (750 ml) Panko* or seasoned breadcrumbs
vegetable oil

Method

Mix first 9 ingredients and 1½ cups (375 ml) Panko crumbs in large bowl. Cover mixture and refrigerate 1 hour. Place remaining 2 cups (500 ml) Panko on large plate. Form scallop mixture into balls, using 1 heaping tablespoon for each. Coat in crumbs, flattening slightly. Heat enough vegetable oil in heavy large skillet over medium-high heat to come ¼ inch up sides of pan. Working in batches, sauté scallop cakes until golden and cooked through, about 2 minutes per side. Transfer scallop cakes to paper towels to drain then to platter and serve. These can be made 4 hours ahead, covered and kept in refrigerator. Reheat on baking sheet at 350°F (180°C) for 8 minutes.
Makes about 40 cakes.

Most scallops are shucked manually by hand at sea and only the meat is brought ashore on ice or already frozen. Shucking scallops at sea and redistributing the shells over scallop beds benefits the scallop fishery. Shuckers (openers and cleaners) call small scallops 'beans' and large ones 'marshmallows.'

Curried Scallop Cakes

Garlic Scallops (Isle of Man)

Ingredients

1 pound (500 g) sea scallops
1 medium sized onion, finely diced
4 to 6 cloves of garlic, finely chopped or crushed
1 tbsp. olive oil
½ cup (125 ml) table cream
4 spring onions, sliced on an angle
splash of white wine
1 tbsp. finely chopped chives or parsley

Method

Sauté garlic and onion with oil in a medium-hot pan for 2 minutes; don't allow to turn colour. Add scallops and lightly cook on one side for 30 seconds. Continue to cook for another 30 seconds and then remove from pan. On medium to high heat, add the splash of white wine to pan and reduce for 1 minute. Add cream and reduce until the sauce thickens to a nice coating consistency. Add scallops and spring onions and gently toss in sauce until mixed. Place garlic scallops on big mound of rice pilaf and pour over sauce, then garnish with chives or parsley.
Makes 4 to 6 servings.

Niarbyl, By permission Isle of Man Government

Steam Railway

Jumbo Scallops in Chimichurri Sauce and Pasta (Caribbean)

Ingredients

2 tbsp. olive oil
1 pound (500 g) jumbo sea scallops
(sized at under 10 per pound)
¼ cup Chimichurri Sauce*
2 tbsp. of each - red, yellow and
green bell pepper (capsicum), finely
diced
8 ounces (250 g) angel hair pasta
(see recipe below)
fresh ground white pepper and salt
as needed

Fresh Angel Hair Pasta

1 tbsp. salt
3 tbsp. olive oil
1 tbsp. garlic, fresh, minced
4 tbsp. butter, cold cut into ¼ inch
(½ cm) slices
3 tbsp. scallion tops, sliced
1 tsp. fresh thyme leaves chopped

Chimichurri Sauce

1 tbsp. olive oil, extra virgin
1 tbsp. lemon juice, fresh squeezed
1 tbsp. lime juice, fresh squeezed
½ tsp. sugar
2 tsp. fresh garlic, minced
1 tbsp. each: fresh cilantro, parsley
 and scallions, finely chopped

Method

Prepare the Chimichurri Sauce and the fresh angel hair pasta as described below. Season scallops lightly on both sides with fresh ground white pepper and salt. Heat the olive oil in a large sauté pan over medium heat until hot but not smoking. Add the scallops and sear on each side for 2-3 minutes until rich golden brown. Remove scallops from pan to avoid over cooking while plating.

In a large sauté pan, heat the olive oil over medium heat, add the garlic and sauté for 1 minute, do not brown. Remove from heat and swirl in the butter until melted then mix in the scallions and thyme. Cook the pasta in the boiling salted water per the instructions on the package. Drain thoroughly in a colander, then add to the scallion-garlic-thyme butter mixture and toss to coat. Cover to keep hot. Mound the hot pasta in the center of two warm dinner plates and add scallops to the pasta. Top each scallop with 2 tsp. of Chimichurri Sauce and a sprinkling of the three colour pepper mix. Season with white pepper and salt.
Makes 4 servings.

Measure and combine all ingredients in a small glass bowl and set aside. Use this sauce with seared, broiled or barbecued scallops. It is also delicious with shrimp and white fish. The ingredients can be doubled or tripled and the extra sauce stored in refrigerator.

Marigot, St. Martin

King Scallops with Ginger-Lime Butter (England)

Ingredients

18 King scallops approximately 2 pounds (1 kg)
2-3 tbsp. olive oil
1 package romaine lettuce
zest and juice of 1 lime
sea salt
freshly ground black pepper

Ginger-Lime Butter

1 inch (2 cm) piece ginger root, peeled and grated
zest of 1 lime plus juice of ½ lime
½ cup (125 g) unsalted butter, softened
freshly ground black pepper

Method

Take the washed scallops straight from the fridge, dry them on kitchen towels and season. Heat a heavy-based pan until very hot and add the oil. Fry the scallops for 1-2 minutes on each side, being careful not to overcook, as this could make them rubbery. Cut the ginger and lime butter into pieces and toss in the pan with the scallops. Arrange the romaine on individual serving plates and place 3 scallops on each. Pour the juices from the pan and the remaining lime juice over the scallops, garnish with lime zest and serve immediately.

To create the ginger and lime butter, place the ginger root, lime zest and juice, butter and seasoning in a food processor and blend until the butter is smooth. Place the mixture in the center of a piece of grease-proof paper or clingfilm, roll up and chill until needed. The ginger and lime butter is best made in advance so that the flavours infuse. You can make it the day before but it will keep for up to 2 weeks in the fridge.
Makes 6 servings.

Sweet, white and all meat, scallops are a shellfish delicacy that are enjoyed around the world. You can enjoy them on every continent, breaded and fried at a coastal fish shack, or sautéed in virgin sauce with a glass of wine at a white-tablecloth restaurant far from the ocean.

The InterContinental, London, UK

King Scallops with Ginger-Lime Butter

Lemon-Apple-Ginger Sea Scallops (New York)

Ingredients

12 fresh sea scallops
2 Granny Smith apples, cored and raw quartered
1 1-inch piece of fresh ginger, peeled and grated
zest and juice of one lemon
1 bunch fresh chives, chopped
1 ounce (30 g) candied ginger, diced
¾ cup (200 g) extra virgin olive oil
Kosher salt, to taste

Method

Combine grated lemon juice, apples and ginger in a food processor and pulse until smooth and the consistency of apple sauce. Season with salt, to taste, and reserve in the refrigerator. Combine the candied ginger, chopped chives and lemon zest in a small bowl and reserve.

To plate and serve, divide the scallops into four servings of 3 scallops each. Place the scallops in the center of a small dish or scallop half-shell. Top each scallop with a half teaspoon of the apple puree mixture, a few drops of olive oil, and then sprinkle with the chive mixture. Serve immediately.

Makes 4 servings.

Lemon-Apple-Ginger Sea Scallops

Marinated Shrimp and Scallops (Caribbean)

Ingredients

1 tbsp. vegetable oil
1 pound (500 g) sea scallops
1 pound (500 g) large shrimp,
peeled and deveined
1 large diced bell pepper (red or
yellow, or combination of both)
1 medium red onion minced
3 tbsp. thinly sliced green onions

Marinade:
4 tbsp. orange juice
2 tbsp. lime juice
1 tbsp. extra virgin olive oil
1 tbsp. Caribbean jerk seasoning
1 tsp. basil leaves

Method

Heat vegetable oil in a large skillet over high heat; add scallops to hot pan and sear 1½ to 2 minutes per side. Transfer scallops to medium bowl and chill. Sauté shrimp in same pan 4 minutes or until shrimp turn pink. Transfer shrimp to another bowl and chill. Combine marinade ingredients in a large bowl. Add chilled shrimp, bell pepper, red onion, and green onions. Cut chilled scallops into quarters; add to bowl; toss well. Cover and refrigerate for at least 1 hour.
Makes 4 – 6 servings.

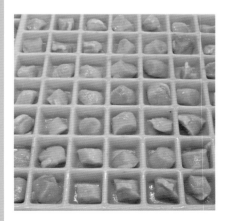

Refrigerate immediately after purchase, and ideally scallops should be cooked or consumed within one day. Scallops may be poached before freezing in their own stock and stored in the freezer for up to three months. Flash-frozen scallops are also available in grocer's freezer cases. It's best to cook scallops briefly via sautéing, grilling, broiling or poaching as over-cooking makes them tough and rubbery. Bay scallops are excellent eaten raw in such foods as sashimi, ceviche or sushi (hotate gai).

Entrees and Main Dishes

Soufriere, St. Lucia

Tasmanian Micro-Waved Scallops (Australia)

Ingredients

½ pound (250 g) scallops
1 tbsp. butter
1 tbsp. finely chopped onion
1 tbsp. of lemon juice
¼ tsp. salt
2 leaves of dried marjoram
dash of paprika (pinch)
6 tbsp. white wine
½ cup (125 g) fresh mushroom
thinly sliced
3 tbsp. flour
3 tbsp. butter
½ cup (125 ml) cream
finely chopped parsley

Method

Place butter and onion in a deep casserole dish. Heat uncovered in microwave for 1 minute or until onion is tender. Add scallops, lemon juice, salt, marjoram, paprika and white wine. Stir to combine and heat in microwave, covered, on high for 2 minutes. At this time scallops should be only slightly cooked. It is easy to overcook the scallops at this step if your microwave is too powerful. Add mushrooms and cook covered on high for 2 minutes. Drain liquid and reserve. Melt the butter in a small bowl on high for 30 seconds, blend in the flour. Gently stir in the reserved scallop liquid and cream. Heat uncovered on medium high for 4 minutes or until thickened and smooth; stir in parsley. Combine the reserved scallop mixture, sauce and the scallops, then place in four serving dishes or scallop shells (great for presentation.) Heat for 4 minutes in microwave on medium-high OR heat for 1 minute in microwave on medium-high and then place under broiler to brown.
Makes 4 servings.

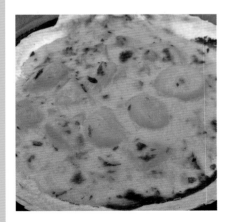

If you want to fish for scallops, make sure that you are familiar with the rules and regulations. A recreational scallop licence is usually required; seasons, size, bag and possession limits apply and there are area restrictions.

Salamanca Place Waterfront, Hobart, Tasmania

Pan Fried Scallops with Lentils (England)

Theo Randall at the InterContinental, London

Ingredients

12 large cleaned scallops
1 red chilli
1½ garlic cloves
2 sprigs of flat leaf parsley
1 sprig sage
1 lemon
½ cup (100g) lentil de Castellucio (Italian lentils)
2 pounds (1 kg) cima di rape or Swiss chard
salt and pepper
1 tsp. fennel seeds

Method

Blanch the cima di rape in salted boiling water until the leaves are tender. Drain. Fry ½ clove sliced garlic with one tsp. fennel seeds and a pinch of dried chilli. Add the cima and stir to combine. Season with salt and pepper.

Boil the lentils until cooked through with one clove garlic and a sprig of sage. Drain off the water, season and add a good dash of olive oil.

Heat a heavy based frying pan. Toss the scallops in a bowl with salt, pepper and olive oil. When the pan is very hot place each scallop in the pan carefully and cook for one minute each side until golden brown. Add chilli, parsley and a squeeze of lemon. Serve on a plate with the lentils and braised cima di rape.

Makes 4 servings.

Advice from a chef: Treat them like miniature tenderloins. They have such a great texture and flavour that they don't need much help.

Theo Randall at the InterContinental, London

Pan Fried Scallops with Lentils

Red and Green Sautéed Scallops

Ingredients

1½ pounds (750 g) large sea scallops, side muscles removed
coarse kosher salt
4 tbsp. extra-virgin olive oil, divided
4 large green onions, chopped, white and green parts separated
1 12-ounce (350 g) container cherry tomatoes or grape tomatoes
4 tbsp. coarsely chopped fresh Italian parsley, divided
3 tbsp. fresh lemon juice
½ tsp. mild Spanish paprika or Hungarian sweet paprika

Method

Rinse and drain scallops; pat dry with paper towels. Sprinkle with salt and pepper. Heat half the oil in large skillet over medium-high heat. Add scallops; sauté until browned outside and just opaque in center, about 2 minutes per side. Transfer scallops to plate; cover. Add 1 tablespoon oil to same skillet; add white parts of green onions and sauté until almost tender, about 1 minute. Add tomatoes and green parts of onions and sauté until tomatoes begin to burst and release juices, about 5 minutes. Stir in 3 tablespoon parsley, lemon juice, and paprika. Return scallops and any accumulated juices to skillet and stir just until heated through, about 1 minute. Season with salt and pepper. Transfer scallop mixture to platter. Drizzle with remaining oil and sprinkle with the parsley.
Makes 4 servings.

The attractive shells of scallops have always interested people. Greeks, Phoenicians and Romans used the scallop shell form on coins, burial urns and for decorative patterns in architecture. At Pompeii, it is found as a wall and floor decoration.

Red and Green Sauted Scallops

Risotto de Scallops (Italy)

Ingredients

1 cup (250 g) Arborio rice
3 cups (750 ml) fish, chicken or vegetable stock
¼ cup (75 ml) diced onion
2 tbsp. olive oil
1 tbsp. garlic butter
½ cup (125 ml) Prosecco or other sparkling wine
¼ cup (75 ml) tomato sauce
¼ cup (75 ml) grated parmesan
¼ cup (75 ml) cream
1 pound (500 g) bay scallops or sea scallops cut in pieces
¼ pound (125 g) lobster meat
1 tbsp. chopped basil
Parmigiano cheese

Method

Sauté onion in olive oil until translucent, add rice to coat. Gradually add warm stock in ½ cup increments, until absorbed, stirring constantly. When just al dente, remove from heat. Sauté garlic butter until browned; add sherry, tomato sauce and cream, salt and pepper to taste. Add scallops and lobster, cover and simmer on low until just cooked. Stir seafood into rice; finish with basil and grated Parmigiano cheese.
Makes 8 servings.

Most sea scallops (Placopecten magellanicus) sold in the U.S. are wild-caught by boats that use dredges. In dredging for scallops, chain-and-nylon mesh bags, shaped like large suitcases, are towed behind the boat to pick up scallops.

Italian houses are as colourful as their foods.

Scallop Crepes (Nova Scotia)

Ingredients

Crepe:
2 eggs
1 cup (250 ml) milk
½ cup (125 ml) water
½ tsp. salt
1 cup (250 ml) all purpose flour
3 tbsp. melted butter

Scallop Filling

1 pound (500 g) bay scallops
6 tbsp. butter
2 tbsp. olive oil
2 tbsp. chopped fresh summer savory
salt and pepper to taste.
3 tbsp. all-purpose flour
1 onion, cut in thin half circles
2 cloves minced garlic
½ cup (125 ml) white wine

Method

Combine ingredients and blend or whisk until smooth. Cover and set aside in the refrigerator for at least 30 minutes, and preferably overnight. Heat a medium sized crepe pan and brush it with a little butter or oil once hot. When it sizzles, pour in a scant ¼ cup ((75 ml) of the batter. Pour directly in the center of the pan and keep pouring in the same spot. Immediately swirl the batter in the pan to spread it around the whole bottom of the pan. Cook for about 1-2 minutes until the bottom of the crepe is golden brown. Turn and let the crepe cook on the second side just until set, about 30 seconds to 1 minute. Place it on a plate in a warm oven while you finish the batch. The first crepe probably won't come out well but taste it to check for salt levels in the batter and adjust seasoning to taste.

In a large skillet, melt the butter, add olive oil and heat until butter foams. Add summer savory, garlic and onions and cook until translucent. Stir in flour until well thickened. Season with fresh pepper and cook about 2 minutes. Add scallops to pan and stir. Sauté over medium heat about 45 seconds. Add white wine and stir well, scraping the bottom of the pan. When the scallops are just about done, remove from heat and let stand for 45 seconds. The sauce will thicken and the scallops will finish cooking from carryover heat. Season to taste. Place a portion of the scallop mixture on each crepe and fold over like a taco. You may grate parmesan cheese over the top and serve with lemon wedges.
Makes 2 – 4 servings.

Thistle Down Country Inn, Digby, Nova Scotia, serves delicious Scallop Crepes for breakfast.

Scallop Brochettes with Maple Syrup Marinade (Quebec)

Yannick Ouellet, Gaspe Bay, Quebec

Ingredients

Method

Marinade:
1 French shallot, thinly sliced
¼ cup (60 ml) maple syrup
2 tbsp. (30 ml) fresh mint, diced
½ cup (125 ml) olive oil
¼ cup (60 ml) rosé wine
1 tbsp. (15 ml) lemon zest
1 tbsp. (15 ml) Dijon mustard
sea salt to taste
pepper to taste

Brochettes:
1½ pound (700 g) large fresh scallops
8 pieces red onion
8 pieces zucchini
8 canned baby corns
8 cherry tomatoes

Combine marinade ingredients in bowl and set aside in refrigerator to cool. Prepare vegetables and scallops. Soak wooden skewers in water for 1 hour so they won't burn. Thread 4 to 5 scallops on each skewer alternately with vegetables. Place in hermetically sealed dish or plastic bag that is air-tight; pour in marinade; cover dish and let marinate for 1 hour in refrigerator. Turn dish several times to allow brochettes to soak up marinate evenly. Heat barbecue or skillet; brush with oil. Cook brochettes about 2 minutes per side. Serve on lemon rice pilaf or seasonal salad. Drizzle brochettes with marinade. Season and serve. If using a skillet, deglaze pan with white wine and maple syrup. Add cream to pan and stir sauce until thickened.
Makes 4 servings.

Photo by Yannick Ouellet, Gaspe Bay.

Cap Alright Lighthouse, Photo by Ghislain Boudreau

New France Festival in Quebec City

Scallop Pasta

Ingredients

½ cup (125 ml) dry white wine
½ cup (125 ml) chicken stock
2 shallots, minced
1 clove garlic, minced
1 tomato, peeled, seeded and diced
2 tsp. (10 ml) tomato paste
pinch powdered saffron
1 ½ pound (750 g) scallops
1 tbsp. (15 ml) cornstarch
½ cup (125 ml) cream
salt and pepper
12 oz. (375 g) pasta, cooked
¼ cup (50 ml) chopped fresh
parsley

Method

Combine wine, chicken stock, shallots, garlic, tomato, paste and saffron in a skillet. Over medium heat, bring to a simmer and cook for 2 minutes. Add scallops and cover and simmer for 3 minutes or until scallops are opaque. With a slotted spoon, remove to bowl; keep warm. Dissolve cornstarch in 1 tbsp. (15 ml) of the cream and add to skillet along with remaining cream. Cook, stirring until boiling and thickened. Return scallops to skillet, stirring to coat. Season with salt and pepper to taste. Spoon over pasta and sprinkle with parsley.
Makes 4 servings.

Scallops, along with various other foods have been held in the highest regards as aphrodisiacs historically. It is easy to see the sexual attraction of scallops. Their flesh is far milder than many of the ocean's creatures. Their texture is soft - voluptuous on the tongue. Their shells make beautiful serving vessels, and, when served at their freshest, scallops offer a flavour that is the essence of the briny sea.

Scallop Pasta

Scallop Quesadillas (Argentina)

Ingredients

1½ pounds (750 g) cooked scallops,
4 oz. (125 g) cream cheese
(Philadelphia)
4 oz. (125 g) pepper jack cheese,
shredded
¾ cup (175 ml) dried fruit* chopped
finely
3 green onions, chopped
¼ cup (75 ml) cilantro, chopped
finely (optional)
2 tbsp. lime juice
¾ cup (175 ml) smoked almonds,
chopped
Tabasco sauce, salt and pepper to
taste.
10 to 12 medium flour tortillas

Method

Combine and mix well all ingredients except scallops. Add scallops and mix gently. Coat ½ of a tortilla with an even ½ -inch layer of scallop mixture. Fold tortilla in half and gently press two sides together. Repeat this process with a second tortilla. Spray sauté pan with vegetable spray and place both folded tortillas in pan, OR very lightly brush each side of folded tortilla with mayonnaise. Cook on both sides until browned. Remove from pan and cut each quesadilla in 4 equal pieces. Arrange on plate and serve with your favorite fresh salsa. Scallops can be seared in butter and lemon juice or dipped in oil and broiled for about 4 minutes.

*dried fruit options: pineapple rings, golden raisins, apricots, mango, cherries, papaya, cranberries.

Makes 6 - 8 servings.

Beach at Villa Gesell, Argentina.

Scallops, Shiitake Mushrooms and Prosciutto

Ingredients

12 fresh shiitake mushroom caps
4 tbsp. olive oil
½ cup (100 g) prosciutto, chopped into very thin strips
½ jalapeno pepper, seeds removed
½ pound (250 g) fresh scallops sliced in half
3 tbsp. clam juice
salt to taste
endive leaves, cleaned and washed

Method

Cut mushrooms into 4 or 6 pieces and cook in skillet with 3 tablespoon of olive oil. Add prosciutto, jalapeno and clam juice. Continue cooking for another 5 minutes. Remove from the skillet and set aside. In the same skillet, add scallops with 1 tablespoon of olive oil and caramelize quickly by turning heat to medium-high. Reduce heat to low and add mushroom mixture and mix well. Season with salt and let mixture warm for 1 or 2 minutes, stirring constantly.

Serve in endive leaves as appetizers. As an entrée, arrange on a serving plate and heat in oven preheated to 375°F (180°C) for about 3 minutes. For a complete meal, add ¼ cup (50 ml) cream (15%) to mushroom - scallop mixture and toss with cooked linguine. Sprinkle with finely chopped coriander and serve with steamed broccoli. Makes 2 – 4 servings.

Portion size: Sea scallops are the largest scallop, with shells up to 9 inches (23 cm) across and meats up to 2 inches (5 cm) across. A typical portion of diver scallops is one to three meats, making them rather affordable, even at $20.00 US per pound ($44.00 per kg.) Bay Scallops are about one third of that price and Sea Scallops just over one half. Generally the larger the scallop, the higher the price.

Scallop, Shiitake and Prochiutto

Scallops and Artichokes

Ingredients

1 pound (500 g) fresh or frozen sea scallops
¾ cup (225 ml) water
1 tbsp. cornstarch
¼ tsp. finely shredded lime peel
1 tbsp. lime juice
1 tsp. sugar
1 tsp. instant chicken bouillon granules
pinch of pepper
9 ounces (300 g) frozen or canned artichoke hearts
1 tbsp. cooking oil
½ cup (125 ml) green sweet pepper, cut into thin strips
½ cup (125 ml) red sweet pepper, cut into thin strips
2 cups (500 ml) cooked couscous or rice
finely shredded lime peel (optional)

Method

Thaw scallops, if frozen. Cut any large scallops in half and set aside. To make sauce, in a small bowl stir together water, cornstarch, ½ tsp. lime peel, lime juice, sugar, bouillon granules, and pepper. Set aside. Run cold water over artichoke hearts until partially thawed. Cut any large artichoke hearts in half. Set aside.

Pour cooking oil into a wok or large skillet and preheat over medium-high heat. Add more oil as necessary during cooking. Stir-fry artichoke hearts and green and red sweet peppers in hot oil for 2 to 3 minutes or until peppers are tender-crisp. Remove vegetables from the wok. Place half of the scallops in the hot wok and stir-fry about 2 minutes or until scallops turn opaque. Remove scallops from the wok and repeat with remaining the scallops. Return all scallops to the wok. Push scallops from the center of the wok. Stir sauce and add it to the scallops. Cook and stir until thickened and bubbly. Return cooked vegetables to the wok. Combine all ingredients to coat with sauce. Cook and stir for 1 to 2 minutes more or until heated through. Serve immediately over hot cooked couscous or rice. Sprinkle with finely shredded lime peel, if desired.
Makes 4 servings.

The US has been France's largest supplier of scallops for the past few years. Most US scallops exported to France are frozen but quantities of fresh scallops have increased. Argentina is the leading US competitor.

Beach at Villa Gesell, Argentina. Photo Courtesy of Sylvia Tseng

Artichokes in Flower

Scallops and Serrano Ham (Spain)

Ingredients

2 cups (500 ml) drained and finely chopped canned whole tomatoes or prepared tomato sauce
½ cup (125 ml) finely chopped drained pimientos
½ cup (125 ml) dry white wine
½ cup (125 ml) fish stock or clam juice
2 pounds (1 kg) bay scallops or sea scallops cut in smaller pieces
¼ cup (75 ml) cognac
¼ cup (75 ml) chopped parsley
½ cup (125 ml) Spanish olive oil
1 large onion, finely chopped
4 cloves garlic, finely chopped
¼ pound (250 g) finely chopped Serrano* ham
salt to taste

Method

Heat the oil over low heat in a large saucepan until fragrant. Add the onion and garlic and cook for 5 minutes, stirring until tender. Add the ham and cook, stirring, for 2 minutes. Add the tomatoes, pimientos, wine, and stock and raise the heat to medium high to bring to a boil. Reduce the heat to low immediately and simmer for at least 10 minutes, partially covered, until the mixture has thickened. Add the scallop pieces and continue to cook for 4 to 5 minutes until done but still tender. Remove the scallops from the sauce and transfer to a heated platter. Finally, to the sauce, add the cognac, parsley, and salt, bring mixture to a boil over medium high heat, pour over the scallops. Serve immediately with warm crusty bread.
Makes 6 to 8 servings.

Scallop farming does not harm the environment and they actually help to replenish the natural stocks. They require no artificial feeding, no chemicals for cleaning and no antibiotics to combat disease but they require clean water to grow and can only be harvested from clean waters. Scallops can be farmed inconspicuously, thus reducing the impact from the shore in scenic areas.

Scallops and Serrano Ham

Scallops Sautéed with Dulse and Nori (Nova Scotia)

Chef Claude AuCoin, Digby Pines Resort

Ingredients

28 large fresh sea scallops
1 ounce (25 g) ground dulse* flakes (available in most supermarkets in Nova Scotia) or toast regular dulse and crumble
3 nori sheets (sushi-type dried seaweed sheets)
½ tsp. freshly ground white pepper
¼ cup (75 ml) olive oil
3-10 inch (25 cm) bamboo skewers that have been soaked overnight in water

Method

In a 350° F (180° C) oven, toast the nori on a sheet pan until dry and it turns slightly brown. Grind into small flakes and mix with the dulse flakes. Skewer the scallops, flat sides against each other as tightly as possible, 8 to 10 scallops per skewer. Season lightly with fresh ground white pepper then roll them in the seaweed flakes. Sauté the scallops on high in a preheated pan with 2 tablespoons olive oil. Roll the skewers in the pan to ensure they are evenly cooked all around. It should take about 4 to 5 minutes and the scallops should be cooked only halfway. To serve, remove the scallops from the skewers and serve either whole or cut in half.
Makes 6 to 8 servings.

Claude AuCoin, Executive Chef at Digby Pines Resort in Nova Scotia, says that really fresh scallops shrink vertically and expand horizontally but regular scallops do the opposite.

Chef Claude AuCoin, Digby Pines Resort

The Digby Pines Resort serves some of the best scallops in the world

Scallops and Avocado Tarts (Norway)

Ingredients

½ sheet of frozen puff pastry
3 corks
½ zucchini
4 very large scallops (8-10's) rinsed in cool water
½ avocado
3 tbsp. (50 ml) olive oil
juice of 1 lime
1 ounce (25 g) parmesan cheese
chopped chives
½ head curly leaf lettuce
½ box of arugula
½ box of red leaf lettuce
½ bunch chives, chopped
2 ounces (50 g) grated parmesan cheese
zest of 1 lime plus juice of ½ lime
3 tbsp. (50 ml) olive oil
salt and pepper, sea salt, chives, olive oil

Method

Roll out the pastry dough on a floured work table. Cut into 4 rectangles of about 4 by 1 inches (10 by 2 cm) and place them on a greased baking sheet. Cut the corks in half and distribute them around the baking sheet. Grease the underside of another baking sheet and place this on the corks. (This is done so that the crusts will rise evenly and be evenly baked - the underside of the baking sheet must be greased so that the pastry dough does not stick.) Bake the tart bases at 400° F (200° C) for about 15 minutes. Cool.

Slice the zucchini and blanch it in boiling water for 2 minutes. Remove to paper towel. Cut the avocado in four pieces, remove the peel, and chop it finely. Make an avocado tartare with chopped avocado, olive oil, a little lime juice, 1 ounce (25 g) grated parmesan cheese and some chives. Slice each scallop horizontally into four pieces.

Make the lime vinaigrette by mixing the grated rind of the lime, the juice of ½ lime and the olive oil together. Season with salt and pepper. Carefully wash and dry all the lettuce. Mix the lettuce and chives and toss with a little of the lime vinaigrette just before serving. On each piece of pastry, place one layer of avocado tartare. Alternate a layer of zucchini slices and a slice of scallop - repeat four times. Place the dressed salad on plates and set the tart on the bed of lettuce; sprinkle each tart with parmesan cheese, coarse salt and chives. Drizzle with a little olive oil and finish with a few drops of the lime vinaigrette.
Makes 4 servings.

Tromso, Norway

Scallops with Pancetta and Vierge Sauce (Mediterranean)

Ingredients

3 ounces (75 g) sliced pancetta
(bacon, cured not smoked)
1–2 tbsp. extra virgin olive oil
16 large scallops, without roe
2 tbsp. unsalted butter

Sauce Vierge

2 tbsp. red wine vinegar
1 large shallot, finely chopped
2 garlic cloves, finely chopped
2/3 cup (150 ml) olive oil
4 vine tomatoes, cored, deseeded
and diced
4 fresh basil leaves, roughly torn

Method

Place the pancetta in a large non-stick pan, overlapping the slices if necessary. Over medium heat, fry the pancetta in its own fat until it is crisp. Remove and drain on kitchen paper. Quickly replace the unwashed pan on high heat and add the oil. It should cover the base with a fine film.

Dry the scallops thoroughly on kitchen paper towel and season. When the pan is very hot, add the scallops in a single layer and cook them in two batches. Press the scallops down with a palette knife to help colour them. After 1 minute, turn them over and cook them for another 2 minutes; add the butter halfway through. The scallops should be firm but still juicy in the middle; longer cooking will make them tough. Transfer scallops to 4 warmed plates, drizzle the Sauce Vierge round them and balance a few strips of pancetta on top. Serve immediately.

To make the sauce vierge, pour the vinegar into a small bowl and stir in the shallot and garlic. Leave to marinate for at least 2 hours, and up to 12 hours. About 30 minutes before the sauce is needed, whisk in the olive oil, then stir in the diced tomatoes and the basil. Season with salt and pepper. This is excellent with fish and other shellfish as well as scallops.

Makes 4 servings.

Night Dining

Scallop - Wild Rice Pie

Ingredients

1 2/3 cups (400 ml) all-purpose flour
½ tsp. salt
1/3 cup (75 ml) cold butter, cut into pieces
1/3 cup (75 ml) shortening
5 tbsp. ice water
2 tbsp. butter
½ pound (250 g) sliced mushrooms
1 large shallot, minced
1 pound (500 g) sea scallops, drained well and cut in quarters
1 tbsp. cornstarch
¼ cup (50 ml) Riesling or other white wine
¾ cup (175 ml) whipping cream
1/3 cup (75 ml) freshly grated parmesan cheese
½ cup (125 ml) cooked wild rice
½ cup (125 ml) chopped hazelnuts
¼ tsp. salt
1/8 tsp. lemon-pepper seasoning

Method

Pulse first 3 ingredients in a food processor 3 or 4 times or until combined. Add butter and shortening, and pulse 5 or 6 times or until crumbly. With processor running, gradually add 5 tablespoons water, and process until dough forms a ball and separates from sides of bowl, adding more water if necessary. Cover and chill.

Melt 2 tablespoons butter in a large skillet over medium-high heat. Add mushrooms and shallot; sauté 5 minutes or until mushrooms are tender. Remove mushroom mixture from skillet; set aside. Add scallops to skillet; sauté 3 minutes. Remove with a slotted spoon; set aside. Whisk together cornstarch and wine in a bowl. Combine cornstarch mixture, cream, and cheese in a large skillet over medium heat; cook 3 minutes or until mixture is thickened. Remove from heat; stir in mushroom mixture, scallops, rice, and remaining ingredients. Set aside and keep warm.

Divide dough in half and roll out each half on a lightly floured surface. Place one half of dough in bottom of a lightly greased 2-quart casserole dish. Spoon scallop mixture over crust. Place other half of dough over filling, pinching to seal edges. Cut slits in top of crust with a knife. Bake at 350°F (180°C) for 1 hour or until crust is lightly browned. Let stand 10 minutes before serving.
Makes 6 to 8 servings.

Scallop-Wild Rice Pie, almost ready for the oven

Scallop-Wild Rice Pie in a Hazelnut Crust

Seafood Lasagna

Ingredients

1 green onion, finely chopped
2 tbsp. vegetable oil
2 tbsp. plus ½ cup (125 ml) butter
or margarine, divided
½ cup (125 ml) chicken broth
8-ounce (250 ml) bottled clam juice
1 pound (500 g) bay scallops
1 pound (500 g) uncooked small
shrimp, peeled and deveined
8-ounce packaged (250 g) imitation
crabmeat, chopped
¼ tsp. white pepper, divided
½ cup (125 ml) all-purpose flour
1½ cups (175 ml) milk
½ tsp. salt
1 cup (250 ml) whipping cream
½ cup (125 g) shredded parmesan
cheese, divided
lasagna noodles, cooked and
drained

Method

In a large skillet, sauté onion in oil and 2 tablespoons butter until tender. Stir in broth and clam juice; bring to a boil. Add the scallops, shrimp, crab and 1/8 tsp. pepper; return to a boil. Reduce heat; simmer, uncovered, for 4-5 minutes or until shrimp turn pink and scallops are firm and opaque, stirring gently. Drain, reserving cooking liquid; set seafood mixture aside. In a saucepan, melt the remaining butter; stir in flour until smooth. Combine milk and reserved cooking liquid; gradually add to the saucepan. Add salt and remaining pepper. Bring to a boil; cook and stir for 2 minutes or until thickened. Remove from the heat; stir in cream and ¼ cup parmesan cheese. Stir ¾ cup white sauce into the seafood mixture.

To assemble lasagna, spread ½ cup white sauce in a greased large baking dish. Top with layer of noodles; spread with half of the seafood mixture and 1¼ cups (300 ml) sauce. Repeat layers of noodles, sauce and parmesan cheese. Bake, uncovered, at 350° F (180° C) for 35-40 minutes or until golden brown.
Let stand for 15 minutes before cutting.
Makes 12 servings.

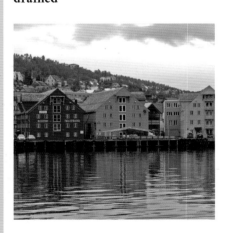

Fiskeriforskning, a research and development company for the fisheries and aquaculture industries in Tromso, Norway, has discovered an enzyme in the Iceland scallop that might prove important in human medicine. This enzyme destroys bacteria associated with infectious diseases in humans and in fish.

Photo courtesy Barbara Ramsay Orr

Seafood Lasagna

Sea Scallop Brochettes (Greece)

Ingredients

2 tbsp. olive oil, (preferably extra-virgin)
2 large garlic cloves, pressed
1½ tbsp. chopped fresh oregano or
1½ tsp. dried
12 large sea scallops
salt and pepper to taste
1 large lemon, halved lengthwise,
each half cut crosswise into 6 slices
8 bay leaves
4 large bamboo skewers, soaked in
water 30 minutes

Method

Whisk 2 tablespoons olive oil, pressed garlic cloves and oregano in medium bowl to blend. Season with salt and pepper. Add sea scallops and toss to coat with oil mixture. Prepare barbecue (medium-high heat) or preheat broiler. Alternate 3 scallops, 3 lemon slices and 2 bay leaves on each skewer. Grill or broil brochettes until scallops are golden brown and just cooked through, about 4 minutes per side. Transfer brochettes to plates and serve with salad or vegetables and rice.
Makes 4 servings.

Typically, Americans and Canadians eat only a scallop's adductor muscle, the disc-shaped white meat which connects a scallop's tissue to its shell. In most other countries, however, scallops are eaten with the roe attached to the adductor meat. Live scallops, which are eaten whole like clams or oysters, are also increasingly popular.

Sea Scallop Brochettes

Seafood Vol-au-Vent

Ingredients

½ pound (250 g) scallops
1 small can lobster meat or 4 ounces
(100 g) fresh meat
1 tbsp. unsalted butter
½ cup (125 ml) white wine
½ cup (125 ml) heavy cream
puff pastry
1 egg, well beaten
4-6 small shrimp

Method

Lay frozen pastry puffs on a baking sheet. Paint tops with beaten egg before baking in a 350° F (180° C) oven for 10-15 minutes or until golden brown and firm. While the puffs are cooking, place a sauté pan over medium heat, melt butter until it bubbles; add lobster meat. Let it sear for a bit to colour the butter and deepen the flavour. Add the scallops and shrimp; increase heat to a gentle boil and stir to loosen up the pan contents being careful not to break the scallops. Finally, add the cream and gently stir to pull the flavours together. Let mixture reduce to desired thickness, about 1 minute. Pour over puff pastry immediately. Cut the top out of the warm vol-au-vent, and pour the sauce over the pastry. Serve immediately with favourite potatoes and vegetables.
Makes 2 servings.

Seafood in Vol-au-Vent

Scallops and Shrimp Au Gratin

Ingredients

6 tbsp. butter
8 tbsp. flour
3 cups light cream or half-and-half
1 pound (500 g) large scallops
1 pound (500 g) medium shrimp or prawns
4 medium white mushrooms
1 small onion diced
4 minced garlic clove
3 tbsp. butter
½ cup sharp cheddar cheese
2 tbsp. dry sherry
1 tbsp. salt
½ tbsp. pepper
paprika, for good colour on top

Method

Melt butter in medium saucepan over medium-low heat. Stir in flour a bit at a time and cook for two minutes, making certain it does not turn brown. Add cream slowly in a thin stream, stirring constantly until very thick. Set aside.

Sauté onions and garlic in butter over medium heat for 3 minutes. Add scallops, shrimp, mushrooms, salt and pepper (or to taste) stirring to mix well. Scallops and shrimp should be stirred occasionally and will cook quickly. Add sherry and grated sharp cheddar cheese to the scallops and shrimp and stir in, then add cream sauce and mix it well until cheese is melted. Pour into large casserole dish or individual serving dishes, sprinkle with cracker crumbs and paprika and bake at 350ºF (180ºC) for 15 minutes or until golden.

Makes 6 – 8 servings.

The Qualicum Beach or Pacific scallop is the primary species farmed by Island Scallops in British Columbia. This a a hybrid of the Japanese scallop and the native weathervane. It is one of the world's largest and yields plump, beautifully textured, divine-tasting meat. Scallop farming is green and sustainable, and is the way of the future, according to many chefs.

Photo courtesy Island Scallops

Simple Scallops Supreme

Ingredients

2 pounds (1 kg) Alaskan or large
sea scallops
1-10oz. (284 g) can mushrooms,
drained
1-10 oz. (284 g) can cream of
mushroom soup
¼ cup (75 ml) sherry
½ tsp. tarragon
bread crumbs
grated parmesan or Romano cheese

Method

Combine all ingredients except toppings, cutting large scallops in half. Place on individual baking shells or on a shallow rectangular casserole dish. Sprinkle with medium layers of bread crumbs and grated cheese. Bake in a pre-heated oven at 350°F (180°C) for 1 hour.
Makes 6 servings.

The U.S. Atlantic sea scallop fishery is one of the most valuable fisheries in the United States and the most valuable wild scallop fishery in the world. By value, scallop is the third ranked species (behind lobster and crab) in Nova Scotia with its worldwide export market.

Simple Scallop Supreme

Swiss Baked Scallops

Ingredients

2 pounds (1 kg) Alaska scallops
1 lemon
½ tsp. white pepper
½ tsp celery salt
½ stick butter
8 slices real Swiss cheese
fresh parsley
paprika

Method

Place scallops in individual baking dishes or scallop shells. Season with lemon juice, white pepper, celery salt and melted butter. Bake in 350°F (180°C) oven for 15 minutes. Remove from oven and pour off a portion of the excess butter and lemon juice. Place slices of cheese on top of scallops and place under broiler until cheese bubbles - watch carefully or it will burn. Garnish with sprigs of parsley and a sprinkle of paprika.
Makes 4 servings.

Princess Scallops are the choice of restaurants in the Gaspé Bay and Magdellen Islands. They are younger and have reddish-pink shells and creamy-white muscle.

Lacarno, Ticino, Switzerland

Szechuan Scallops (China)

Ingredients

3 capiscum (sweet peppers, red, green, yellow) cut in 1 inch squares
1 large sweet onion, cut in 1 inch cubes and layers separated
2 tbsp. dry sherry or white wine
2 tbsp. light soy sauce
½ tsp. ground ginger
1 tsp. hot red chili flakes or to taste (optional)
2 cups fresh or thawed scallops (about 10 ounces, 275 g)
¾ cup spicy tomato juice

Method

Chop vegetables and arrange all ingredients near stove. Prepare a large nonstick skillet or electric frying pan liberally with cooking spray. Arrange onions in skillet in a single layer. Cook over medium heat just until onion begins to brown. Combine all ingredients, except scallops, in skillet; cover, bring to a simmer, and cook for 5 minutes. Uncover and simmer until sauce thickens - 4 or 5 minutes more. Stir in scallops, and cook just until heated through and coated with sauce. Serve with Szechuan noodles or plain rice.

Makes 4 servings,

Around 96 percent of the scallops consumed in the United States are captured from the wild in U.S. and Canadian fisheries. Of the 4 percent that are farmed, most are imported from China and Japan. While Japan has provided key advances in scallop aquaculture technology, some concerns remain about the cultured scallops raised in China.

Mango Scallops (Singapore)
The Travelling Gourmet

Ingredients

12 large scallops
1 large mango
1 medium Spanish onion
1 medium capsicum (red pepper)
1 clove of garlic finely diced
1 tsp. extra virgin olive oil
1 - 2 tsp. Demerara sugar to taste
1 tbsp. honey or more according to taste
pinch of sea salt
dash of Vietnamese fish sauce from Saigon (or Chinese Soy sauce)
freshly ground pepper
2 tbsp. (30 ml) Prosecco
1 medium size fresh red chili pepper

Method

Cut the mango flesh into paysanne dices (½ x ½ x 1/8 inch). Cut the capsicum into diamond shape lozenges (½ x ½ x 1/8 inch). Fine julienne (1/16 x 1/16 x 1 to 2 inches) the onions and sauté the garlic and onions in a non-stick frying pan. Add the mango, sugar, capsicums, fish sauce and honey. Now add the Prosecco and simmer until the mango is soft but NOT soggy and mushy. Timing is critical at this stage. Add in the scallops. Sauté until just cooked. The inside should be a little raw. DO NOT overcook. Add the fresh ground white pepper to taste. You may adjust the viscosity of the sauce by the reduction or addition of more Prosecco but save some for drinking! Serve immediately garnished with rings of chili pepper.
Makes 3 – 4 servings.

Dr. Michael Lim prepares a dish for Eva Ellinghausen, Razor TV. Michael says the most important thing about preparing scallops is not to overcook them and to be sure to serve a good wine with them.

Photo courtesy Michael Lim

Singapore

Venetian Scallops (Italy)

Entrees and Main Dishes

Ingredients

2 pounds (1 kg) scallops
1 large onion, sliced thin
½ cup raisins
½ cup pine nuts
4 tbsp. butter
3 tbsp. flour
2 cups (500 ml) light cream
salt

Pepperonata

2 red bell peppers (capsicum or paprika)
2 yellow bell peppers
1 medium size onion, sliced
1 crushed clove of garlic
2 tbsp. tomato salsa
2 tbsp. extra virgin olive oil
fresh basil
salt and pepper to taste

Method

Rinse the scallops under cold water. Sauté the sliced onions and the scallops in butter over medium heat until golden brown. Add flour and mix. Add cream, raisins, and pine nuts. Salt to taste. Lower the heat and simmer until reduced by half. Serve with polenta and pepperonata.
Makes 4 servings.

Cut the peppers and onion into big pieces, approximately the same size, so they cook evenly. Begin by cooking the onion over low heat for about 10 minutes until it becomes translucent. Add the garlic, peppers, tomato sauce, salt and pepper. Cook covered for 15 minutes and then about a half hour with the lid removed, over low to medium heat. At the end, before serving, sprinkle with some freshly torn basil.

Wasabi Vol-au-Vent

Ingredients

1 whole sheet of puff pastry
1 large egg
2 tbsp. milk
6 tbsp. mayonnaise
2 tsp. wasabi paste or powder
1 pound (500 g) bay scallops or sea scallops cut in small pieces
2 tbsp. wasabi caviar plus some for garnish (optional)
salt and white pepper

Method

Heat oven to 400°F (200°C.) Defrost pastry dough according to manufacturer's directions. In a small bowl, whisk together egg and milk; set aside. Line 2 baking sheets with parchment; set aside. On a lightly floured surface, use a 1-inch pastry cutter to make 36 rounds. Use the cutter to make indentations on the centers of the rounds without cutting through the dough. Using a pastry brush, coat rounds with egg wash. Cook on prepared baking sheets until raised and golden brown, 10 to 12 minutes. Transfer to a wire rack to cool. Gently push the indented center into the cavity and remove to form a shell. If necessary, use a paring knife to coax out the center. Level the bottom with a paring knife so the shell won't wobble. Repeat with the remaining shells.

In a large bowl, mix together mayonnaise, wasabi paste and scallop meat. Gently fold in caviar. Season with salt and pepper; refrigerate until ready to serve. To serve, fill pastry shells with scallop-caviar mixture; garnish with more caviar.

Makes 8 servings.

The word scallop comes from the Old French escalope meaning "shell," referring to the shell that houses the scallop. Scallops are mentioned in print as far back as 1280, when Marco Polo mentions scallops as being one of the seafoods sold in the marketplace in Hangchow, China.

Conversion Chart

For cooking purposes only

Small Measures

1/4 tsp.	= 1 ml
1/2 tsp.	= 2 ml
3/4 tsp.	= 4 ml
1 tsp.	= 5 ml
1 tbsp.	= 15 ml
2 tbsp.	= 30 ml

Liquid Measures

1/4 cup	= 60 ml
1/3 cup	= 75 ml
1/2 cup	= 125 ml
2/3 cup	= 150 ml
3/4 cup	= 175 ml
1 cup	= 250 ml
4 cups	= 1000 ml (1 litre)

Weight Measures

1/4 pound	= 125 g
1/3 pound	= 175 g
1/2 pound	= 250 g
3/4 pound	= 375 g
1 pound	= 500 g (1/2 kg)
2 pounds	= 1000 g (1 kg)

Glossary

Glossary of terms in this book

- AL DENTE: cooked but not soft or overdone
- ARBORIO RICE: Italian-grown, high-starch rice with short, fat grain
- ARUGULA: a slightly bitter, aromatic salad green with a peppery mustard flavour; also called rocket, roquette, rugula and rucola
- AU GRATIN: any dish that is topped with cheese or bread crumbs mixed with bits of butter, then heated in the oven or under the broiler until brown and crispy
- BACON LARDOONS (Lardons): bacon that has been diced, blanched and fried
- BISQUE: a thick, rich soup usually consisting of pureed seafood (sometimes fish, seafood, fowl or vegetables) and cream
- BLANCH: to plunge food (usually vegetables and fruits) into boiling water briefly, then into cold water to stop the cooking process
- BLINI: see CREPE
- BOURBON: an all-American liquor distilled from fermented grain, named for Bourbon County, Kentucky
- BROCHETTES: refers to food cooked on a skewer
- CAPISCUM: any plant-bearing fruits called peppers red, orange, yellow or green sweet pepper
- CARPACCIO: thin shavings of raw meat or fish served as an appetizer
- CAVIAR: sieved and lightly salted fish roe (eggs)
- CEVICHE, SEVISHE: an appetizer consisting of very fresh, raw marinated fish
- CHILLI, CHILI, CHILE PEPPERS: hot peppers
- CHOWDER: any thick, rich soup containing chunks of food including seafood, fish and corn
- CIMA DI RAPE: a popular green from Puglia, Italy, similar to sprouting turnip tops; flavour between turnips and broccoli; eat the florets, leaves and stalk
- COCKLES: common name for a group of small, edible, saltwater clams
- CONFIT: generic name for various foods that have been immersed in a substance (i.e. oil) for flavour and preservation, sealed and stored in a cool place; can last for several months
- CORAL: the roe (eggs) of a crustacean such as lobster or scallop; when cooked, it turns a beautiful coral-red colour
- COTIJA OR AÑEJO CHEESE: Mexican cheeses similar to parmesan or Romano
- COULIS: a thick puree or sauce
- CREPE: French word for pancake, light, paper-thin and filled
- DREDGE: to lightly coat food to be fried with flour, cornmeal or bread crumbs to help brown the food
- DRY-CURED: a process of rubbing ham with salt, letting it cure then air-drying or smoking

- DULSE: an edible red-purple seaweed harvested around the North Atlantic
- EMPANADAS: a stuffed bread or pastry
- FOIE GRAS: the enlarged liver from a goose or duck that has been force-fed and fattened over a period of 4 to 5 months
- FRITTERS: any kind of food coated in batter and deep fried
- HOT CHILLIES: jalapeno, chipotle, habenero, pasilla, chili negro (fresh hot green chillies that turn black when dried)
- JERK SEASONING: a dry seasoning blend; generally a combination of chillies, thyme, spices (such as cinnamon, ginger, allspice and cloves), garlic and onions
- JULIENNED: cut in narrow strips
- JUS: French word for "juice," which can refer to both fruit and vegetable juices, as well as the natural juices from meat
- LAVERBREAD: a traditional Welsh seaweed that is harvested, cleaned, cooked and minced to a paste
- MADEIRA WINE: a fortified Portuguese wine made in the Madeira Islands, often used for cooking
- MAPLE SYRUP: sap from maple trees that has been boiled until most of the water has evaporated and becomes thick and syrupy; produced in Canada and north-eastern United States
- MARINADE: a seasoned liquid in which meat, fish or vegetables are soaked to absorb flavour and tenderize; made from an acid such as wine, lemon or lime juice, herbs and spices
- NORI: paper-thin dried seaweed sheets used for wrapping sushi; often toasted; very rich in protein, vitamins, calcium, iron and other minerals
- OPAQUE: not transparent or translucent; turning white
- PANCETTA: an Italian bacon that is cured with salt and spices but not smoked; comes in a sausage-like roll
- PEPPERONATA: stewed peppers; there are innumerable variations
- PESTO: an uncooked sauce made with fresh basil, garlic, pine nuts, parmesan or pecorino cheese and olive oil; the ingredients can either be crushed with mortar and pestle or finely chopped with a food processor
- PIMENTOES: the Spanish word for pepper; large, red, heart-shaped pepper; the red stuffing found in green olives; found in cans and jars as well as fresh
- POLENTA: a mush made from cornmeal; can be eaten hot with a little butter or cooled until firm, cut into squares or slices and fried
- POMELO: giant citrus fruit native to Malaysia related to the grapefruit
- PROSECCO: an Italian dry sparkling wine made from a variety of white grape of the same name; the grape is grown mainly in the Veneto Region
- PUREE: to grind or mash food until completely smooth by using a food processor or blender or by forcing the food through a sieve
- QUESADILLAS: a corn, wheat or flour tortilla that is filled; quesadillas are cooked after being filled or stuffed, while a taco or burrito is filled with pre-cooked ingredients
- REDUCTION: a mixture obtained from boiling a liquid rapidly until the volume is reduced by evaporation, thereby thickening the consistency and intensifying the flavour
- ROE: a delicacy of fish eggs; the roe of shellfish is called coral while the roe from fish such as sturgeon and salmon, is known as caviar

- SALSA: Mexican word for sauce; can range in spiciness from mild to mouth-searing; salsa cruda is uncooked salsa; salsa verde is green salsa
- SALSIFY: biennial herb of the family Asteraceae, native to the Mediterranean; similar to a parsnip; also known as oyster plant
- SAUTÉ: to cook food quickly in a small amount of oil in a skillet or sauté pan over direct heat
- SCALLIONS: the name for members of the onion family including scallion, green onions , young leeks and sometimes the tops of young shallots; true scallions have a mild flavour
- SERANNO HAM : dry-cured ham found at Hispanic markets; can substitute Prosciutto, Brasola, Bayonne or Westphalian ham
- SHUCK: to remove the edible part of the scallop or oyster from its shell
- SIDE MUSCLE: the small, smooth muscle attached to the adductor muscle; edible and tasty but a bit tougher; usually whiter than the main adductor meat
- SUMMER SAVORY: (Satureja hortensis) the traditional herb in Atlantic Canada, where it is used in the same way sage; known as Bohnenkraut in Germany
- SUNCHOKES: known as Jerusalem Artichokes; a nutty, sweet and crunchy vegetable with white flesh; can be eaten raw in salads or cooked by boiling or steaming and served as a side dish or in soup
- SWEET POTATO: large edible root, native to tropical America; darker variety has a thick, dark orange skin and a vivid orange, sweet flesh that cooks to a moist texture; sometimes called yams but they are not related
- SZECHUAN: a mildly hot spice native to the Szechuan province of China
- TABASCO: fiery sauce made in Louisiana from tabasco peppers, vinegar and salt; fermented in barrels for 3 years before being processed into the sauce;
- TARTARE: dish of coarsely ground or finely chopped high-quality, raw lean beef, fish or seafood
- TEQUILA: a colourless or pale straw-coloured liquor made by fermenting and distilling the sweet sap of the agave cactus plant; originated in Tequila, Mexico
- TOMATILLOS: a plant related to tomatoes and eggplant; green or green-purple fruit surrounded by a paper-like husk; sometimes called green tomatoes
- TORTILLAS: a very flat, round, thin bread make from wheat or corn flour and cooked on a hot rock or skillet
- VIERGE: French sauce made from olive oil, lemon juice, tomatoes, and basil
- VOL-AU-VENT: light puffed pastry; can be purchased in frozen-food section of supermarket; means flying in the wind
- WASABI: the Japanese version of horseradish made into a green-coloured condiment that has a sharp, pungent, fiery flavour
- WILD RICE: long-grain black seeds from marsh grass native to the northern Great Lakes area of North America; known for its luxurious nutty flavour and chewy texture
- YAMS: a root, similar in size and shape to sweet potatoes; yams contain more natural sugar and have a higher moisture content; not as rich in vitamin C and A as sweet potatoes

INDEX

About the Author

If you walk Canada's coastline, and you are fit enough to cover 20 km. a day, it would take you exactly 33 years to complete your journey. That is about the same time Judy Eberspaecher has taken to collect, create, taste and organize the recipes along with her research in this book. With 243042 kilometers of coastline, the longest in the world, Canada is a natural choice for seafood. Having grown up close to the sea, some of Judy's earliest memories of foods are of scallops, brought to the door by the local fish peddlers. Eating scallops and collecting recipes, not only from Canada but virtually every corner of the world from Alaska to Australia, Judy presents recipes from some of the finest chefs and establishments worldwide. An accomplished travel and nature photographer, Judy (Hiltz) Eberspaecher lives in Canada but spends much of her time travelling with her husband Alex, a wine and travel writer, in her search for the perfect dish. You might even find her out on a scallop dragger doing research alongside scientists and local fishermen. Judy belongs to professional travel journalists organizations and can be reached at www.eberimage.ca.

Photo by Gary Crallé